The
Colossal
COLUMBO
Quiz Book

The
Colossal
COLUMBO
Quiz Book

****

A Plethora of Perplexing
Questions About Television's
Greatest Detective Show

---

by ALAN L. GALPERT

ABOUT THE COVER: If you are wondering what the Leaning Tower of Pisa has to do with COLUMBO, it is simply that both the landmark and the Lieutenant are Italian.

The Colossal COLUMBO Quiz Book
Copyright © 2013 by Alan L. Galpert

ISBN-13: 978-1492800644
ISBN-10: 1492800643

Printed in USA by CreateSpace

DEDICATION

This book is dedicated, with love, to my parents, Alvin and Lois Galpert. Dad is no longer with us, I am sad to say, but he was a COLUMBO fan, also. Mom prefers opera. They both liked bridge.

GRATITUDE

My sincere thanks to Gary Jacobs for his crackerjack proofreading skills, sage editorial judgment, helpful suggestions, and encouragement when it was badly needed.

Many thanks to my wonderful daughter, Rachel Adcock, who urged me to complete this project; and to my wonderful son, Alan, who provided emotional support.

CONTENTS

PREFACE

I hope that those of you who know all the answers in this book will, at least, find it entertaining.

I hope that those of you who know none of the answers will find it enlightening.

I hope that for both of you (and everyone else), it rekindles your love for the show, enhances your appreciation of it, and inspires you to watch episodes you may not have seen before, or to watch again those you have already seen.

THE FORMAT

I have endeavored to make this book as user-friendly as possible. The answers are neither at the end of the quizzes, where you might see them accidentally (not because you would cheat), nor at the end of the book, where it is inconvenient. Also, whenever possible, the NBC and ABC episodes are divided into two quizzes (or listed separately in the same quiz), for the benefit of readers who may have seen only the shows on one network – that is not unlikely, given the lengthy hiatus between the two series.

The quizzes are rated for difficulty with exclamation points (like chili peppers on the menu at a Mexican restaurant). The ratings range from no exclamation points to three. Three exclamation points means: "Caution: This Quiz May Be Hazardous to Your Ego." The ratings are a general guide, and should not be taken too seriously – everybody has a different knowledge base.

A NOTE ON PETER FALK'S BOOK

Many of the anecdotes related in the "PETER FALK" quiz were gleaned from his autobiography (the title of which won't be revealed here, because there is a question on it). Anyone interested in the actor or the show is well advised to read it. Maybe the publisher won't take me to task (or court) for quoting from the book, if I plug it – but that isn't the reason for my doing so. It is funny, poignant, candid and engagingly written. (It isn't ghost-written, either, as many Hollywood autobiographies are.) Quite a few photographs, and a number of Falk's own delightful sketches augment the book's value.

OTHER RECOMMENDATIONS

Surprisingly, there is only one book besides this one (that I know of) about the show – fortunately, it is great one. It is called THE COLUMBO PHILE (admirable title – a pun, in keeping with the episode titles), and was written by Mark Dawidziak, who is a newspaper journalist, a college professor, and a prince of a human being. Prior to embarking on this writing venture, I searched Amazon for any books that might be useful, and I discovered Mark's. That was the good news. The bad news was that used copies were going for several hundred dollars, minimum. I might (if I had the money) pay that for a first edition of THE GREAT GATSBY, but I couldn't justify that kind of money for a book by an unknown author, nor could I understand it. I wrote to Mark, inquiring if he had any extra copies, and requesting an explanation for the prohibitive cost of his book. As busy as Mark is, he replied immediately, and at considerable length. He explained in detail about "piracy on the Internet high seas," and regretted that he didn't have an extra copy (for both our sakes). But he did have it on a flash drive, which he sent me posthaste. That would have been quite enough, but he wouldn't let me pay for it, either – not even the postage.

Mark spent several weeks in Hollywood hobnobbing with people connected to the show, from producers and directors to guest stars. There are many behind-the-scenes anecdotes, and a detailed commentary about every episode that aired on NBC. That is the only downside (besides the prices) – the book was written before the second incarnation of the series, so the later shows are not included. Mark is a fine writer, and a witty fellow. So keep your eyes open – you may get lucky and come across a copy at a rummage sale. If not, there is always a chance that it might be available for Kindle someday. (And don't forget your local library.)

I also want to recommend STAY TUNED, which was written by Richard Levinson and William Link about their lives and careers. There is only one chapter (albeit a long one) on COLUMBO, but anyone who is interested in the machinations involved in producing programs for network television will be well rewarded by reading it. Used copies are available from Amazon – and the prices are reasonable.

For research purposes, the Internet Movie Database (IMDb.com) has synopses of all the episodes, and a complete list of the cast, writers and directors for every show. The Wikipedia article ("List of COLUMBO episodes") is even better for details of the plots, but not nearly as good for the personnel.

Finally, anyone reading this book would probably enjoy the COLUMBO fan website. It comes from England, and is maintained by several friends of Mark's. The address is: columbo-site.freeuk.com. (Tell them I sent you, and maybe they will promote my book.)

A NOTE TO THE READER

This is the first of two books of quizzes that were planned. Writing it has been a labor of love, but (as they say) love don't pay the bills. Whether or not the second book ever sees the light of day depends on how well this one is received. That, in turn, depends largely on you. If you enjoy the book, and your appetite for all things COLUMBO hasn't been satiated yet, please do whatever you can to help this one along. You will be doing both of us a favor.

Here is a preview of the second book:

1. From five to ten questions about every episode
2. Quotations
3. Recycling Can Be Fun
4. More Red Herrings and Red Flags
5. More Trivia

"And I thank you for your support." (For any readers who might remember the Bartles and James commercials of days gone by.)

A SAD STORY

Not long ago, I tried to organize a COLUMBO convention. There are, as you may know, STAR TREK conventions and I LOVE LUCY conventions, and who knows what else. Unfortunately, my endeavor was ill-fated. As soon as ten middle-aged men with thinning hair, all wearing tan raincoats, showed up in the park on a day when it wasn't raining, some overly zealous citizen called the Vice Squad, and the whole thing fell through (or maybe I should say, "Peter-ed out").*

(* I am kidding, of course.)

FEEDBACK

Reader feedback is welcome. Let's be honest: praise is welcome, and criticism is grudgingly accepted (unless it is positive).

I am interested in the opinions of other COLUMBO fans. Here is a short survey, the results of which will be included in the second volume of this book.

1. What is your favorite episode?

2. Who was your favorite murderer? (An odd-sounding question.)

3. What was your favorite murder method? (Another odd-sounding question.)

4. What was your favorite clue?

5. Is there a quote you are especially fond of?

6. What actor or actress would you have most liked to see as a COLUMBO villain? (He or she does not have to be anyone who could really have been on the program, based on the time frames when it aired.)

7. Do you know of any "goofs" on the show that could be included in the next book?

8. Which do you prefer overall: the NBC episodes, or the ABC episodes?

Please e-mail your answers, or other comments, to: alangalpert@yahoo.com.

INTRODUCTION

COLUMBO was the program you might get if you crossed LIFESTYLES OF THE RICH AND FAMOUS and BARETTA. (Maybe it should have been called HOMICIDES OF THE RICH AND INFAMOUS.) Gone was the underbelly of society. Gone were the denizens of the "mean streets" of America's downtowns. In their place were the occupants of Easy Street, the upper crust: America's aristocracy, without the titles. The people we look up to, instead of down on.

Ironically, the very elements that might have torpedoed the show probably contributed to its success, because they made it stand out from the competition. You have a crime show without any "action," a mystery that (in most cases) is not a mystery, a detective who is hardly a matinee idol, and murderers who are not always evil. COLUMBO was a long shot, but it worked. It not only worked, but many critics have called it the greatest detective show ever on television.

INSPIRED TITLES

The episode titles themselves were worth the price of admission (so to speak):

"Suitable for Framing"
"Dead Weight"
"Murder by the Book"
"An Exersise in Fatality"
"Any Old Port in a Storm"
"Negative Reaction"
"A Stitch in Crime"
"Ransom for a Dead Man"
"The Greenhouse Jungle"
"Mind Over Mayhem"
"Etude in Black"
"Murder Under Glass"
"Death Hits the Jackpot"
"Blueprint for Murder"

A DIFFERENT KIND OF SETTING

Most crimes – on television and in the movies, at least – occur in a rather unsavory milieu. Litter-strewn alleys, warehouses, honky-tonks, red light districts, and blighted downtowns are the familiar backdrop of the typical crime show. But on COLUMBO, those tableaux have been replaced by well-manicured lawns and multi-million-dollar mansions. For ninety minutes (two hours, sometimes) lucky viewers could indulge their fantasies, and live vicariously in opulence.

After watching other crime shows, an episode of COLUMBO gives one the distinct feeling of having passed, like Alice, through the looking glass.

A DIFFERENT KIND OF DETECTIVE SHOW

The contrast between COLUMBO and most other crime-fighting shows is striking. For all intents and purposes, MAGNUM, P. I. and COLUMBO are two different genres -- not just two types of detectives. You could enjoy reading an episode of COLUMBO, but not one of MAGNUM or MIAMI VICE. COLUMBO is a thinking person's detective show. The good Lieutenant's weapons are his eyes, his ears and his brain -- not a gun (which he didn't even know how to shoot), and certainly not his fists.

Relatively few television shows appeal to either the emotions or the intellect, and almost none satisfy both. COLUMBO is that rare program that challenges the mind and can also stir the soul. A few episodes may be a little weak on plot; several others may not be quite up to par on clues; and a couple might lack plausible motives. But I can't think of one that isn't worth watching.

In passing, I will note that the titles of shows about character cops invariably use just their name -- in most cases, only one name. It is somewhat surprising that the highly creative people who originated them didn't use a little more imagination. But at least you knew what you were getting.

A DIFFERENT KIND OF PLOT

The most obvious difference is the format. A mystery program has to be a "whodunit," right? If you know who the guilty party is, what is left? Plenty, as it happens. Whether you call it an "inverted detective story," or a "police procedural," the fascination (not the Devil) is in the details. What will lead to the killer's downfall? Is he/she going to trip himself/herself up, or is Columbo going to have to trick him/her somehow? COLUMBO is like the game of "Clue" brought to life. It is a puzzle to solve, as much as a drama to watch.

A DIFFERENT KIND OF DETECTIVE

To find Columbo's soul-mate at the time the show aired, one had to look outside of television. He resembled Sherlock Holmes and Hercule Poirot more than any television detectives at that time, whether they were policemen or private investigators. That soon changed, however, largely due to the success of COLUMBO. In the wake of its popularity, detective series became nearly as commonplace as Westerns were in the 1950s, or spy shows in the 1960s. Following Lt. Columbo, so-called "character cops" became the newest genre of heroes: Barnaby Jones, Cannon, Kojak and Baretta, to name a few. (In spite of the name, they weren't all cops – and some weren't entirely heroic.)

In the annals of television crime-fighting, Lt. Columbo is almost unique. With few exceptions, private detectives are lone wolves. They stalk their prey by themselves, possibly with the help of one or two operatives, who may or may not be on the payroll. In contrast, police detectives invariably hunt in packs. The cast lists of shows like BARNEY MILLER and HILL STREET BLUES read like the phone book of a small town. Like them, Columbo is a police detective, but he works alone. A revolving door of Sergeants, and an occasional Lieutenant, render assistance from time to time, but Columbo is essentially a one-man-band. The two networks that aired the series strongly believed that Columbo should have a side-kick, but the producers steadfastly resisted the idea. The closest they came to acquiescing was giving him a dog, whose usefulness in solving crimes was severely limited. Even when he does have a colleague, that person usually hinders more than he or she helps. Not being as astute as Columbo, they accept the "obvious" solution to the murder, and roll their eyes at his misgivings. They only tolerate his questions and heed his demands because they are his subordinates.

One thing noticably absent from COLUMBO are the clashes with superiors that we typically see in this genre. McCloud is habitually browbeaten by Chief Clifford. Quincy and Monahan are forever crossing swords. On the other hand, Columbo's Captain is often mentioned but (almost) never seen. Like his relatives, who are also never seen, he might not even exist (except that he is seen once, in "No Time to Die"). He could be merely a creative means of getting Columbo 'off the hook'. He often tells suspects that it is the Captain who wants these impertinent questions answered "for my report" – he himself wouldn't be so gauche. The closest that Columbo comes to interdepartmental friction is the impatience we perceive in his underlings, who are at pains to understand what is bothering him, or what he is looking for.

Humorist Elaine May is credited with saying that "Columbo is an ass-backward Sherlock Holmes." That is very funny, but not very accurate. The two men are certainly different in appearance, and to some extent, in personality. But they are still the same type of detective. Professionally, they are quite similar, and that is the important thing. Elaborating on Ms. May's comment, Falk (in his autobiography) contrasts the two detectives in three ways. He says:

a. Holmes has a long thin neck; Columbo has no neck.

b. Holmes speaks the King's English; Columbo is still working on his.

c. Holmes wears tailor-made British tweeds; Columbo's coat should be cleaned and burned.

That last line ("Columbo's coat should be cleaned and burned") is actually a quote from the show, attributed to Mrs. Columbo.

A recently popular detective show is called MONK. He is almost always referred to in the media as a detective with Obsessive-Compulsive Disorder. I haven't seen the program, so I can't comment on what type of OCD the man has. But I can tell you that Columbo has a healthy (or unhealthy) dose of it, as well. People are inclined to think of those who have it as being abnormally tidy and organized. A perfect example is Agatha Christie's Hercule Poirot, who had a full-blown case of the disorder long before Monk was a gleam in some television producer's eyes. "Tidy and organized" does not describe Columbo, to be sure. But he does obsess over small details in the case, a tendency which works well to his advantage. While he may not be orderly in appearance, his mind certainly is.

His idiosyncracies, including his OCD, contribute to his likeableness. The false exits, the pensive pauses, his inability to keep track of a pen or pencil, his continual search for a place to deposit his eggshells. (Speaking of false exits, I believe that every episode should have been limited to two "Just one more thing"s. After that, it becomes annoying not only to the suspect but also to the viewer.) Many people prefer their heroes to be supermen, especially in the arena of crime-fighting (understandably). Columbo is not a superhero in the traditional sense, although his feats of detection can be awe-inspiring. But being just an average Joe is what makes him relatable, and comfortable, like an old friend.

Columbo's car – a rolling advertisement for the virtue (if not the wisdom) of recycling – is a natural extension of his less-than-heroic persona. In the ABC episodes, it can be seen that the car not only looks bad, but is barely functioning. It backfires, rattles, and the breaks squeal. (The last trait is of questionable veracity, as it wouldn't pass inspection, and it is a cop's car, after all). I would call this a perfect illustration of Shakespeare's phrase, "gilding the lily." In other words, enough is enough. We get it, already.

Columbo's wardrobe, his demeanor, and his intellect all contribute to the appeal of the character, but I believe that one other quality is even more important. What makes Columbo so endearing (and enduring) is that he takes his job seriously, but never himself. He is devoted to justice, and cares deeply about the victims – even the more sympathetic villains. But unlike many other detectives, he doesn't consider himself God's gift to women, or the last word in crime-fighting, or the toughest hombre on the block. He is just doing his job. (Sometimes we do get the impression that Columbo thinks he might be the world's greatest detective, but he isn't arrogant about it. Let us say he has healthy self-esteem.)

A DIFFERENT KIND OF INVESTIGATION

Columbo doesn't beat confessions out of his suspects. He doesn't overpower them – he "underwhelms" them. Someone has said that a Columbo investigation is "like being nibbled to death by a duck." The game of cat-and-mouse is even more fun to watch than seeing bad guys get beaten to a pulp.

Columbo's method compares favorably with the technique of a judo master. A judo practitioner uses his opponent's strength against him. Columbo doesn't always use this approach, but he frequently puts ideas into his suspects' heads, and then waits for them to trip themselves up. That way, he gets the results he wants with relatively little effort on his part.

A DIFFERENT KIND OF CRIMINAL

The killers on the show are <u>thinking</u> criminals, and resourceful ones; they are not your garden-variety gangsters and dope dealers. From a moral standpoint, that doesn't matter. A killer is a killer, after all. But we can admire their minds, and wish we were that clever. Their intelligence comes into play in many ways (not all of which apply in every case): in the design of the murder; in the creation of an alibi or a frame-up; in the covering up of their tracks, when things go awry; or in the invention of plausible explanations for their incriminating behavior.

Just as important, why did he or she do it? Motive takes a back seat (if it is present at all) in most mysteries, because we don't know who the murderer is. You have to know the <u>who</u>, before you can learn the <u>why</u>. Motive is really the program's third dimension. The villains in other crime shows are just that: villains. They wear black hats. The miscreants on COLUMBO do bad things, but many of them are not bad people. Even the ones who are bad people, or who have egregious motives, are partly redeemed in our eyes by their intelligence.

In a few episodes, we almost feel sorry for the murderers when they are arrested, either because they seem so pitiful (Ruth Lytton and Adrian Carsini), or because their motive is so understandable (Abigail Mitchell). In other situations, while we don't have any sympathy for the killer or his motive, his

17

scheme is so ingenious and so painstakingly executed, that it doesn't seem fair that he is caught – especially when his undoing is caused by a small and unforeseeable detail. Our sense of justice is satisfied, but our sense of fair play is not.

A FEW THEORIES

Not long after COLUMBO premiered and had, surprisingly, become a phenomenon, speculation began. When a show that shouldn't have succeeded did just that, the pundits asked themselves how it could have happened. Karl Marx claimed that class struggle is the primary cause of history. Could this account for the popularity of COLUMBO, too? After all, here you have a poorly attired, and probably poorly paid, journeyman cop – a working class hero, if ever there was one – going toe to toe with the elite of society, and bringing them down. A reasonable test of that hypothesis would be to analyze demographic data from the 1970s this way: gather viewership numbers from the Nielsen ratings, and plot them against income figures from the IRS. If anyone reading this feels like doing that, please let me know what you find out.

Staying with the socio-economic interpretation, there is the soap opera syndrome. Some critics claim that one reason for the popularity of soap operas is that viewers who are not rich and beautiful see that people who are rich and beautiful have the same problems they do, or worse. They get cheated on, too; and their loved ones develop brain tumors, too. It is undoubtedly easier for us to accept our straitened circumstances when we see that people who seem to have it all may not be as happy or as blessed as we think they are.

On COLUMBO, the insight we are given into the killers' motives helps to humanize them, and they are no longer faceless plutocrats. Even if the motive isn't a sympathetic one – if it is greed or revenge, for example – it is still human. They may be rich and powerful, but they are driven by the same passions as the rest of us.

There is also the character angle. Presumably a large percentage of viewers identified with the blue-collar Columbo, instead of his white-collar adversaries, who are rich, but also corrupt. In contrast, Columbo is relatively poor, but moral, which matched their own self-image. In addition to seeing themselves in Columbo, they might have seen their boss, their doctor, or their lawyer in one of the villains.

Finally, there is the power angle. Many years before Karl Marx was the Bible, which tells the story of David and Goliath, a tale that has inspired underdogs for centuries. Columbo is the "little guy" many people can relate to. If he can beat the mighty at their own game (especially by outsmarting them), maybe there is hope for the rest of us little guys, too.

THE WORLD'S GREATEST SLEUTH?

In interviews, Falk unabashedly touted Columbo as "the world's greatest detective." His enthusiasm is understandable, and he can be forgiven his hyperbole, but he is wrong. The greatest television detective? Probably – on network television, anyway. But he isn't in the same league with Hercule Poirot, Sherlock Holmes, Nick Charles, Inspector Maigret, or most of the other sleuths in literature and on film.

Poirot's cases, in particular, are considerably more complex and puzzling. He never has fewer than three or four legitimate suspects, all with compelling motives and no alibis. Columbo usually has only one real suspect, and possibly another who is framed. His challenge is seeing through whatever deception the guilty party has arranged for the police. The deceptions are often ingeniously crafted, but the discovery of only one incongruity (what I call a "red flag" in a quiz devoted to them) confirms that something is wrong. The incongruity does not, by itself, incriminate the villain – but it does exculpate the framee (coined word), or put the lie to the botched robbery, kidnapping, or apparent accident. Like a house of cards, if you pull one out, the whole edifice crashes to the ground. Once he is on the right track, Columbo has only to look for more evidence, or rattle the suspect's cage until he/she reveals himself/herself or confesses.

Columbo gets lucky, too. For example, one murderer is undone primarily because a drunk happens to be in the junkyard when he kills his accomplice. The derelict hears the shots, and his testimony doesn't agree with the killer's account of what happened. In another episode, the killer takes pains to ensure that the victim isn't identifiable, but as he is carrying the body to the beach, a book connecting the two men falls out of the victim's pocket. Real cops do get lucky sometimes, so there is truth value in that, but their powers of deduction aren't tested when it happens.

19

If I didn't love Columbo (the show, the character, and the actor who portrays him), I wouldn't have written this book. But I also know where he ranks in the pantheon of the greatest fictional detectives.

IDLE SPECULATION

It is somewhat of a mystery why the creators of COLUMBO made their character a cop. They claim that they were inspired by British drawing-room mysteries, but those books had little action (unlike cop shows), and usually private detectives. (The latter was true then, but is less so now – on television, anyway.) One of the few precedents for a detective show was DRAGNET, a realistic police drama that was a far cry from COLUMBO. It is true that one of their models for the character was a policeman, but the other was not. Besides that, Columbo dresses in civilian clothes, drives a civilian car, and almost never visits the squad room.

The primary reason may have been that since he is a policeman, suspects have to talk to him. The arrogant and insular killers on COLUMBO probably wouldn't deign to talk to a private investigator – especially one who looks, talks and acts like Columbo. One other possibility is that he benefits occasionally from the findings of the crime lab and (less often) the police database, which are usually off-limits for private eyes.

PART ONE

GENERAL QUESTIONS

QUIZ 1.1: The SHOW

QUIZ 1.2: The KUDOS

QUIZ 1.3: PETER FALK

QUIZ 1.4: LT. COLUMBO

QUIZ 1.1: The Show (!!)

1. COLUMBO was created by:
   a. Steven Bochco
   b. Alfred Hitchcock
   c. Stephen J. Cannell
   d. William Link and Richard Levinson

2. Which of these scenarios describes COLUMBO'S history?
   a. It was a Broadway play, then a movie, then a TV series.
   b. It was a TV episode, a play, a pilot, then a TV series.
   c. It was a movie, then a TV series.
   d. It was a Broadway play, then a TV series.
   e. It was an original series written for television.

3. What label best describes the show's format?
   a. Whodunit
   b. Police procedural
   c. Inverted detective story
   d. Retroactive inquiry
   e. Situation comedy

4. On what networks did COLUMBO air?
   a. NBC first, then ABC
   b. CBS first, then ABC
   c. ABC first, then NBC
   d. NBC first, then CBS

5. In what years did the original primetime series begin and end its run (excluding the first pilot episode)?
   a. 1968–1982
   b. 1969–1979
   c. 1975–1985
   d. 1971–1979

6. For how many years was the show on hiatus before it was picked up by another network?
   a. 9
   b. 10
   c. 12
   d. 14

7. What was the title of the first pilot episode?
   a. "Murder by the Book"
   b. "Dead Weight"
   c. "Prescription: Murder"
   d. "Lady in Waiting"

8. What was the title of the second pilot episode?
   a. "Ransom for a Dead Man"
   b. "Try and Catch Me"
   c. "Publish or Perish"
   d. "A Matter of Honor"

9. What is the title of the premiere episode in the first season?
   a. "Short Fuse"
   b. "Suitable for Framing"
   c. "Murder by the Book"
   d. "Death Lends a Hand"

10. What is the title of the last NBC episode?
    a. "How to Dial a Murder"
    b. "Last Salute to the Commodore"
    c. "The Bye-Bye Sky High IQ Murder Case"
    d. "The Conspirators"

11. What are the last words Columbo utters at the end of the seventh season?
    a. "This far, and no farther."
    b. "Well, Sergeant, that about wraps things up."
    c. "I'm taking Mrs. Columbo dancing tonight at the lodge."
    d. "I'm headed home for a nice bowl of chili and a hot bath."

12. To whom was the role of Columbo offered before Falk?
    a. James Garner
    b. Bing Crosby
    c. Robert Wagner
    d. Lee J. Cobb

13. How many Academy Award winners starred on the show (in any role)?
    a. 8
    b. 9
    c. 11
    d. 13

14. How many of them play murderers?
    a. 5
    b. 7
    c. 9
    d. 10

15. Which Oscar winner owned the most golden statuettes?
    a. Edith Head
    b. Ray Milland
    c. Anne Baxter
    d. Celeste Holm

16. True or False? Peter Falk is the only actor who played Columbo on the show.

17. How many total episodes of COLUMBO were broadcast?
    a. 50
    b. 75
    c. 69
    d. 46

18. What was the highest number of episodes in a regular season?
    a. 10
    b. 8
    c. 9
    d. 7

19. What was the lowest number of episodes in a regular season?
    a. 3
    b. 4
    c. 5
    d. 6

20. What was the title of "Prescription: Murder" in its first incarnation on THE CHEVY MYSTERY SHOW?
    a. "Enough Rope"
    b. "Murder by Death"
    c. "Diagnosis: Murder"
    d. "Diagnosis: Terminal"

21. COLUMBO was produced by what film studio, which still owns the rights to it?
    a. Paramount
    b. 20th Century Fox
    c. Universal Studios
    d. Columbia Pictures

22. The first six seasons were broadcast under what banner?
    a. THE NBC MYSTERY MOVIE
    b. MASTERPIECE THEATER
    c. THE CHEVY MYSTERY SHOW
    d. PLAYHOUSE 90

23. The series was shown, originally, in a rotation with what two other shows? (The networks call this arrangement a "wheel.")
    a. BANACEK
    b. McMILLAN AND WIFE
    c. TENAFLY
    d. McCLOUD
    e. CANNON

24. The majority of COLUMBO episodes run how long?
    a. 60 minutes
    b. 30 minutes
    c. 120 minutes
    d. 90 minutes

25. Who wrote the NBC Sunday Mystery Movie theme music?
    a. Henry Mancini
    b. Burt Bacharach
    c. Marvin Hamlisch
    d. Bernard Herrmann

QUIZ 1.2: The Kudos (!!!)

1. How many Emmy nominations did Peter Falk receive for COLUMBO?
   a. 5
   b. 6
   c. 8
   d. 10

2. How many Emmy Awards did Falk <u>win</u> for COLUMBO?
   a. 2
   b. 3
   c. 4
   d. 5

3. COLUMBO was nominated for how many Emmy Awards?
   a. 15
   b. 21
   c. 27
   d. 38

4. How many total Emmy Awards did the show <u>win</u>?
   a. 7
   b. 10
   c. 13
   d. 15

5. How many Emmy nominations did the show receive in Acting categories?
   a. 8
   b. 10
   c. 11
   d. 14

6. How many Acting Emmys were <u>won</u> on the show?
   a. 3
   b. 4
   c. 7
   d. 8

7. How many guest stars were nominated for Emmy Awards for their work on the show?
   a. 3
   b. 4
   c. 5
   d. 6

8. Which actor(s) was/were nominated for an Emmy for his/their COLUMBO appearance?
   a. Dabney Coleman
   b. Jack Cassidy
   c. Patrick McGoohan
   d. Robert Culp
   e. Robert Vaughn

9. Only one guest actor won. Who was it?
   a. Jack Cassidy
   b. Robert Culp
   c. Patrick McGoohan
   d. Dabney Coleman
   e. Robert Vaughn

10. Which actress(es) was/were nominated for COLUMBO?
    a. Tyne Daly
    b. Ruth Gordon
    c. Vera Miles
    d. Faye Dunaway
    e. Lee Grant

11. Only one guest actress won. Who was it?
    a. Tyne Daly
    b. Faye Dunaway
    c. Vera Miles
    d. Ruth Gordon
    e. Lee Grant

12. How many Emmy Awards in non-Acting categories did the show win?
    a. 6
    b. 8
    c. 9
    d. 11

13. How many times was COLUMBO nominated for an Emmy for Outstanding Drama Series?
    a. 3
    b. 5
    c. 7
    d. 9

14. How many times did it win?
    a. None
    b. One
    c. Two
    d. Three

15. The writing, directing and acting on COLUMBO are widely recognized as outstanding. But the show also won three Emmy Awards in which of these categories?
    a. Editing
    b. Cinematography
    c. Costume design
    d. Art direction

16. It was nominated for three Emmys in which categories?
    a. Editing
    b. Art direction
    c. Music composition
    d. Costume design

17. The series received two Emmy nominations (winning one) in which category?
    a. Editing
    b. Art direction
    c. Costume design
    d. Camera work

18. The show was nominated once in each of three categories. In which category was it not nominated?
    a. Art direction
    b. Camera work
    c. Costume design
    d. Directing

19. The first season was a banner year for COLUMBO. How
    many Emmy nominations did it receive?
    a. 5
    b. 8
    c. 9
    d. 10

20. How many did it <u>win</u> at the 1972 Emmy Awards?
    a. 2
    b. 3
    c. 4
    d. 5

21. How many Emmy nominations did the show receive for
    the 24 episodes that aired on ABC between 1989 and
    2003?
    a. 7
    b. 10
    c. 11
    d. 15

QUIZ 1.3: Peter Falk (!!)

1. Before becoming an actor, Peter Falk was a:
   a. Lawyer
   b. Certified Public Accountant
   c. Dentist
   d. Truck driver

2. True or False? Falk's real name was Peter Faulk.

3. Falk was born on September 16, 1927, in what city?
   a. New York, N. Y.
   b. Newark, N. J.
   c. Stamford, CT
   d. Richmond, VA

4. True or False? Falk lost one of his eyes at the age of three because of an accident.

5. What is the name of the high school Falk attended?
   a. Brooklyn Heights High
   b. Westhampton High
   c. Ossining High
   d. Stuyvesant High

6. In high school, Falk was:
   a. Editor of the newspaper
   b. Director of the school play
   c. President of the Senior class
   d. Class clown

7. True or False? Falk earned an M. A. in Public Administration at Syracuse University.

8. What was Peter Falk's religious background?
   a. Jewish
   b. Roman Catholic
   c. Episcopalian
   d. Buddhist

9. What rather embarrassing thing happened to Falk when he was 13?
   a. He knocked down a number of women while trying to catch the bouquet at a wedding.
   b. His swim trunks came off at the community pool.
   c. He ran for class treasurer and got only 10 votes.
   d. His voice changed in the middle of a song during choir practice.

10. Falk served in which branch of the service?
    a. Army
    b. Navy
    c. Marines
    d. Coast Guard
    e. None of the above

11. What is the reason Falk was so eager to finish college?
    a. He couldn't wait to start his career.
    b. An American girlfriend was waiting for him in Paris.
    c. He needed money for a car.
    d. He wanted to travel.

12. What four words changed Falk's life?
    a. "Well, you should be."
    b. "How do you explain that?"
    c. "Who's next in line?"
    d. "Take me, for instance."

13. Who said them?
    a. Lee Strassberg
    b. Neil Simon
    c. Eva La Gallienne
    d. His high school drama teacher

14. True or False? Falk worked for the State of Connecticut as an efficiency expert.

15. Falk says he took how long to decide to become an actor?
    a. 5 years
    b. 12 years
    c. 18 years
    d. 9 years

16. What well-known movie producer rejected Falk when he
    arrived in Hollywood, saying: "For the same money, I can
    get an actor with two eyes!"
    a. Sam Goldwyn
    b. David O. Selznick
    c. Jack Warner
    d. Harry Cohn

17. True or False? Three weeks before Castro took over
    Cuba, Falk was mistaken in Havana for a revolutionary,
    and was detained.

18. Falk was how old when he married the first time?
    a. 25
    b. 30
    c. 32
    d. 19

19. How many Academy Awards (Oscars) did Falk win?
    a. Two
    b. Three
    c. None
    d. One

20. True or False? Columbo's famous raincoat was Falk's
    own.

21. What is the title of the first movie for which Falk was
    nominated for an Academy Award?
    a. PRETTY BOY FLOYD
    b. THE BLOODY BROOD
    c. WIND ACROSS THE EVERGLADES
    d. MURDER, INC.

22. He was nominated again two pictures later. What is the
    title of that film?
    a. THE SECRET OF THE PURPLE REEF
    b. POCKETFUL OF MIRACLES
    c. PRESSURE POINT
    d. THE BALCONY

23. True or False? Falk played a gangster in both movies for which he was nominated for an Academy Award.

24. What is the title of Falk's autobiography?
    a. NO REGRETS
    b. JUST ONE MORE THING
    c. CURTAIN CALL
    d. ALL HANDS ON DECK

25. What is the subtitle of the autobiography?
    a. IT COULD'VE BEEN WORSE
    b. I SHOULD'VE KNOWN BETTER
    c. TOO CLOSE FOR COMFORT
    d. STORIES FROM MY LIFE

QUIZ 1.4: Lt. Columbo (!)

1. Columbo and Agatha Christie's Hercule Poirot are alike in which of these respects? (Choose all that apply.)
   a. They are meticulous about their appearance.
   b. They are private detectives.
   c. They are obsessed with small details.
   d. They are happily married.

2. Columbo's favorite expression is:
   a. "Who loves you, baby?"
   b. "Just one more thing. . ."
   c. "Here's looking at you, kid!"
   d. "The plane, the plane!"

3. Columbo's dog is a:
   a. Schnauzer
   b. Basset hound
   c. German shepherd
   d. Pomeranian

4. Columbo's dog's name is:
   a. "King"
   b. "Fido"
   c. "Rex"
   d. "Dog"

5. The dog debuted in which episode?
   a. "Etude in Black"
   b. "Forgotten Lady"
   c. "Playback"
   d. "Try and Catch Me"

6. Which of these activities does the dog enjoy? (Choose all that apply.)
   a. Eating ice cream (vanilla)
   b. Watching television
   c. Chasing cats
   d. Swimming in the neighbor's pool

7. In which episode does Columbo take his dog to a picnic where all the dogs are the same breed?
   a. "Murder in Malibu"
   b. "Murder: A Self Portrait"
   c. "Agenda for Murder"
   d. "Columbo Cries Wolf"

8. True or False? The dog that appears in its first episode is the same dog that appears in its last episode.

9. Columbo drives a:
   a. 1970 Mercedes Benz 450SL
   b. 1959 Peugeot 403 Cabriolet
   c. 1969 Chevy Impala
   d. 1965 Mustang convertible

10. Columbo's car has:
    a. A white convertible top
    b. A silver body
    c. Seen better (far better) days
    d. A desperate need for a tuneup
    e. All of the above

11. The car's license plate number is:
    a. California 044 APD
    b. California APD 044
    c. California CSI 123
    d. California 123 CSI

12. True or False? Columbo never puts the top down on his car.

13. Columbo is known for: (Choose all that apply.)
    a. His rumpled raincoat
    b. His pomaded hair
    c. His flashy ties
    d. His patent leather shoes

14. Columbo is queasy about: (Choose all that apply.)
    a. Sailing
    b. Hospitals
    c. Elevators
    d. Flying
    e. Heights

15. Columbo's favorite food is:
    a. Chili (with crackers)
    b. Chop suey
    c. Pizza
    d. Tournedos Rossini

16. How does Columbo drink his coffee?
    a. Black
    b. Black, with sugar
    c. With cream and sugar
    d. With cream, without sugar
    e. He doesn't drink coffee

17. Columbo is an avid: (Choose all that apply.)
    a. Wine connoisseur
    b. Pool player
    c. Bowler
    d. Scuba diver
    e. Body builder

18. Columbo's unofficial theme song is:
    a. "For He's a Jolly Good Fellow"
    b. "This Old Man"
    c. "Auld Lang Syne"
    d. "Thanks for the Memories"

19. The theme song was introduced in which episode?
    a. "Any Old Port in a Storm"
    b. "Lovely but Lethal"
    c. "Candidate for Crime"
    d. "Double Exposure"

20. True or False? The theme song was ad-libbed (originally).

21. Columbo never: (Choose all that apply.)
    a. Drives recklessly
    b. Apologizes to a suspect
    c. Seems to have a pencil or a match
    d. Forgets what he was going to say
    e. Loses his temper

22. Columbo's first name is:
    a. Peter
    b. David
    c. Frank
    d. Never given

23. Mrs. Columbo is:
    a. A shrew
    b. A tall, sexy blonde
    c. A fat, frumpy brunette
    d. Never seen

24. Columbo and Thomas Magnum have what in common?
    a. A way with women
    b. An athletic build
    c. A fondness for sports cars
    d. Nothing

25. Columbo is:
    a. Retired from the LAPD
    b. A Lieutenant in the homicide division of the LAPD
    c. Of German ancestry
    d. A sharp dresser

ANSWERS
QUIZ 1.1

1. (d) Bochco wrote the teleplay for six episodes, and Cannell wrote one. Alfred Hitchcock had nothing to do with it; he was busy enough already.

2. (b)

3. (b) and (c) are both correct. It is definitely not (a), since we see the murder being committed, and I made up (d).

4. (a) Two-thirds of the episodes were on NBC.

5. (d) The first pilot aired in 1968. The second was shown in March, 1971, and the series began later that year.

6. (b) It ended on NBC in 1979, and began on ABC in 1989.

7. (c) It stars Gene Barry. That was also the title of the play, but not the original television episode.

8. (a) Lee Grant is the star of that one.

9. (c) Jack Cassidy and Martin Milner star.

10. (d) Clive Revill is the murderer. (a) was the penultimate episode. (b) and (c) were the last episodes of seasons 5 and 6, respectively.

11. (a) They were prophetic, as it turned out, because it was the last one on NBC. He learns the line from Joe Devlin.

12. (b) Surely this belongs in the "What were they thinking?" file. Bob Hope, maybe; he, at least, played detectives in the movies. The story goes that Bing thought it would interfere with his golf game. It is nothing personal, but I am thankful that he played golf. Lee J. Cobb was considered, but was never asked. He would have been a good choice, though.

13. (d); 14. (b)

15. (a) She was nominated 35 times for an Academy Award in Costume Design, and won 8.

16. True. However, Thomas Mitchell had the role before he did on the stage. Before that, Bert Freed played him in an episode of THE CHEVY MYSTERY SHOW, which aired 7 ½ years before the first pilot for COLUMBO did.

17. (c)

18. (b) Seasons 2 and 3 both had eight episodes.

19. (a) Season 6, the last one aired as the NBC MYSTERY MOVIE, had only three episodes.

20. (a) Presumably this is taken from the expression, "Give someone enough rope to hang himself."

21. (c); 22. (a)

23. (b) and (d)

24. (d) Later on in the series, 2 hour shows were tried, but the consensus of the producers was that 120 minutes was too long for a show with a lot of talk and little action. (Women reading this will think, "I know men like that.")

25. (a) That is triple what he was earning in the third season.

QUIZ 1.2

1. (d); 2. (c); 3. (d); 4. (c)

5. (d) Peter Falk (10), Patrick McGoohan (2), Faye Dunaway (1), Dabney Coleman (1)

6. (c) Peter Falk (4), Patrick McGoohan (2), Faye Dunaway (1)

7. (b)

8. (a), (c)

9. (c) He actually won twice, for "Identity Crisis" (1975) and "Agenda for Murder" (1990).

10. (d), (e)

11. (b) She won for "It's All in the Game."

12. (a) Cinematography (3), Editing (1), Writing (1) and Directing (1)

13. (b) In 1972, 1973, 1976, 1977 and 1978

14. (a) However, it won an Emmy for "Outstanding Limited Series" in 1974.

15. (b) Lloyd Ahern (1972); Harry Wolf (1974); Richard Glouner (1975)

16. (c) Patrick Williams (1978, 1989); Billy Goldenberg (1972)

17. (a) Won by Edward Abroms in 1972. Robert Watts was nominated in 1978.

18. (b) Grady Hunt was nominated for Costume design in 1973. / Jerry Adams (Set decorator) and Michael Baugh (Art director) were nominated for Art direction in 1975. / Edward Abroms was nominated for Directing in 1972.

19. (d) Out of 38 total nominations for the series.

20. (c) Out of 13 wins for the entire series. It won for Writing (Levinson and Link), Acting (Peter Falk), Editing (Edward Abroms), and Cinematography (Lloyd Ahern).

21. (a) From a critical standpoint, it was far more successful on NBC, where it earned 31 nominations for 45 episodes.

QUIZ 1.3

1. (b)

2. False. But he is credited that way in one of his first films.

3. (a)

4. False. He did lose an eye, but it was from cancer. He was lucky it was discovered in time, and so are we.

5. (c); 6. (c)

7. True. He also held a B. S. in Political Science, from the New School for Social Research in New York City.

8. (a)

9. (a) You can't make this stuff up.

10. (e) He couldn't serve because of his glass eye, but he did join the Merchant Marines for a year-and-a-half.

11. (b); 12. (a)

13. (c) A renowned actress and director, LaGallienne taught a course on Shakespeare in Westport, CT. Attendance was limited to professional actors. Falk lied about being one so he could take the class. He would work his day job in Hartford, then drive to Westport. The third day in a row that he was tardy, LaGallienne asked him the reason. He explained that he had to drive from Hartford. She wanted to know why an actor would live where there were no theaters. He said that he really wasn't an actor, and she replied, "Well, you should be. Now sit down." The next day he quit his job, and the rest is history.

14. True. Can you imagine Columbo as an efficiency expert?

15. (b)

16. (d) He was the head of Columbia Pictures, and was notorious for his boorishness.

17. True. After persuading the authorities that they were in error, he left on the next available flight.

18. (c)

19. (c) He was nominated twice, but lost both times.

20. True. He bought it on 57th Avenue in NYC (in the rain, appropriately enough) to wear in MURDER, INC. Contrary to popular belief, it is not on display at the Smithsonian Institute, but stayed in his closet.

21. (d) It was only his fourth picture.

22. (b)

23. True

24. (b) It doesn't take a rocket scientist. . .

25. (d)

QUIZ 1.4

1. (c) Poirot is famous for his fastidious toilet; Columbo always looks like he just got out of bed. / Poirot is a private detective; Columbo is a policeman. / Columbo is married, apparently happily; Poirot is a life-long bachelor.

2. (b) Returning several times after false exits is quite annoying to Columbo's suspects. (a) is from KOJAK; (c) is from CASABLANCA; (d) is from FANTASY ISLAND.

3. (b)

4. (d) The dog was a pound puppy. Columbo says he doesn't have a name, but he calls him "Dog" (which is somewhat of a contradiction).

5. (a) Despite being a dog lover (he owned six), Falk initially opposed the idea of having a dog, but when he saw it, he knew instantly that it was the perfect complement to Columbo's personality.

6. All except (c). "Phlegmatic" is a good word to describe the animal. He would make the perfect doorstop. (No SPCA calls, please.)

7. (b)

8. False. The first one died. Its replacement was younger, so cosmetics were used to make it look older. Falk says that the dog spent more time in makeup than he did.

9. (b) The original was sold when NBC ceased production, and ABC had to find a replacement when it picked up the series. In "Caution: Murder Can Be Hazardous to Your Health," Columbo says the car is a 1950 Peugeot, but research indicates that that is incorrect.

10. (e); 11. (a)

12. False. In "Columbo and the Murder of a Rock Star," he puts it down during the speeding ticket demonstration.

13. (a)

14. All of them. A pretty neurotic guy, actually.

15. (a)

16. (a) Any true COLUMBO fan would know that the answer isn't (e). Coffee is usually the first thing the Lieutenant asks for when he is called to a crime scene at odd hours. He does drink it black most of the time, but has been known to ask for cream, on occasion.

17. (b) and (c)

18. (b); 19. (a)

20. True. Columbo is waiting on the phone to hear about the weather on a particular day. Since he has nothing to do, he starts humming to himself. In some episodes, the humble tune gets a full symphonic treatment.

21. (c) You might think (e), also, because he is usually calm, cool and collected. But he does lose his composure in a couple of episodes.

22. (c) He is never addressed as such, but in "Dead Weight," "Frank" is visible on his ID badge. If you answered (d) you can still give yourself credit.

23. (d) Mrs. Columbo got her own show when COLUMBO went off the air, but the character wasn't what the creators had in mind originally, and they opposed the show.

24. (d)

25. (b)

PART TWO

BEHIND THE SCENES

QUIZ 2.1: The PRODUCERS

QUIZ 2.2: The DIRECTORS

QUIZ 2.3: The WRITERS

QUIZ 2.1: The Producers (!!!)

1. True or False? Levinson and Link met in the Army during WWII.

2. True or False? Levinson and Link produced the show through the third season.

3. They wrote a book about their television careers which, of course, included a chapter on COLUMBO. What is the title?
   a. STAY TUNED
   b. RIDING THE AIRWAVES
   c. TRAPPED INSIDE "THE BOOB TUBE"
   d. DICK AND BILL'S EXCELLENT ADVENTURE

4. Who took over as Executive Producer after Levinson and Link left?
   a. Richard Alan Simmons
   b. Edward K. Dodds
   c. Dean Hargrove
   d. Roland Kibbee

5. Including made-for-TV movies, how many episodes of programming were Levinson and Link responsible for, either as producers or writers?
   a. 258
   b. 496
   c. 511
   d. 623

6. True or False? The two principal characters in "Murder by the Book" (played by Jack Cassidy and Martin Milner) were loosely based on Levinson and Link.

7. In the first season, Levinson and Link were under the gun to produce six 90-minute episodes (which turned into seven) between March, 1971, when the show was picked up, and September, 1971, because Falk was due to appear on Broadway in what play?
   a. THE PRISONER OF SECOND AVENUE
   b. WAITING FOR GODOT
   c. THE PRODUCERS
   d. A FUNNY THING HAPPENED ON THE WAY TO THE FORUM

8. Richard Levinson won a record how many Edgar Awards from the Mystery Writers of America?
   a. Two
   b. Four
   c. Three
   d. Five

9. True or False? On the whole, the producers loved Falk because he was reliable, but the guest stars didn't like working with him because of his perfectionism.

10. Dean Hargrove was a producer, director and writer on COLUMBO. After leaving the show, what very popular series did he create?
    a. CAGNEY AND LACEY
    b. THE X-FILES
    c. MATLOCK
    d. THE WEST WING

11. He was also the Executive Producer of which of these shows? (Choose all that apply.)
    a. DIAGNOSIS: MURDER
    b. JAKE AND THE FATMAN
    c. FATHER DOWLING MYSTERIES
    d. MURDER, SHE WROTE

12. Levinson and Link wrote only one script besides "Prescription: Murder" (not counting story ideas they contributed). What was it?
    a. "Death Lends a Hand"
    b. "Murder by the Book"
    c. "Dead Weight"
    d. "Short Fuse"

13. Roland Kibbee was a producer and writer on the series. He won an Emmy for COLUMBO, and for what other television show?
    a. THE BOB NEWHART SHOW
    b. MADIGAN
    c. McCOY
    d. BARNEY MILLER
    e. IT TAKES A THIEF

QUIZ 2.2: The Directors (!!!)

Some of Hollywood's best-known directors, in both television and the movies, got their start or advanced their careers, working on COLUMBO. How much do you know about these talented individuals?

1. Who directed the most episodes?
    a. James Frawley
    b. Vincent McEveety
    c. Patrick McGoohan
    d. Harvey Hart

2. Who directed the two pilot episodes?
    a. Richard Irving
    b. Edward F. Abroms
    c. Hy Averback
    d. Robert Butler

3. Who directed the second-most episodes?
    a. Patrick McGoohan
    b. James Frawley
    c. Bernard L. Kowalski
    d. Harvey Hart

4. How many episodes did Peter Falk direct?
    a. Two
    b. Three
    c. Four
    d. One

5. What is/are the title(s)?
    a. "Suitable for Framing"
    b. "Last Salute to the Commodore"
    c. "Blueprint for Murder"
    d. "Fade in to Murder"

6. True or False? Because he was a first time director, the producers gave Falk an easy script to direct.

7. Many years before directing "Lady in Waiting," this versatile actor appeared in two Hitchcock films, and produced and directed episodes of his television shows. From 1982 to 1988, he starred as Dr. Auschlander on ST. ELSEWHERE. What is this nonagenarian's name?
   a. Joseph Cotten
   b. William Daniels
   c. Norman Lloyd
   d. William Holden

8. Ben Gazzara and John Cassavetes were two of Peter Falk's closest friends. Ironically, Gazzara is known mainly as an actor, but he was a director on COLUMBO. Cassavetes is known for directing, but he acted on COLUMBO. Which two episodes did Gazzara direct?
   a. "Etude in Black"
   b. "Troubled Waters"
   c. "Playback"
   d. "A Friend in Deed"

9. He directed the COLUMBO episode "Murder under Glass," but Jonathan Demme is best known for a 1992 film he directed, for which he won an Oscar as Best Director. What was the film?
   a. THE SILENCE OF THE LAMBS
   b. UNFORGIVEN
   c. JFK
   d. SCHINDLER'S LIST

10. He has a long list of credits in television, made-for-TV movies, and theatrically released movies. He directed all 178 episodes of PEYTON PLACE, and two of COLUMBO ("A Case of Immunity" and "A Matter of Honor").
    a. Ted Post
    b. E. W. Swackhamer
    c. Walter Grauman
    d. Hy Averback

11. Which future CHEERS cast member does not appear on screen, but directed two episodes?
    a. Ted Danson
    b. Nick Colasanto
    c. Kelsey Grammer
    d. John Ratzenberg

12. His daughter Katey may be better known to television viewers, but this Ukranian-born director's credits include THE TWILIGHT ZONE, ALFRED HITCHCOCK PRESENTS, and THE MAN FROM U.N.C.L.E., among many other shows. He received four Emmy nominations for the television mini-series RICH MAN, POOR MAN, and directed two episodes of COLUMBO.
    a. Bernard L. Kowalski
    b. Alf Kjellin
    c. Sam Wanamaker
    d. Boris Sagal

13. Which episode(s) did Patrick McGoohan both direct and star in?
    a. "Murder with Too Many Notes"
    b. "Last Salute to the Commodore"
    c. "Agenda for Murder"
    d. "Identity Crisis"
    e. "Ashes to Ashes"

14. Which two COLUMBO alums directed over one-third of the 264 episodes of MURDER, SHE WROTE?
    a. Vincent McEveety
    b. James Frawley
    c. Walter Grauman
    d. Harvey Hart

15. He is another director whose children may be better known than he is. They include a musician and two actors, one of them a double-Oscar winner. He himself began as an actor, but after being blacklisted in the McCarthy witch hunt of the 1950s, he turned to directing. His credits include STAR TREK, ST. ELSEWHERE, I SPY and CAGNEY AND LACEY (among many others), and three COLUMBO episodes.
    a. Jack Smight
    b. Richard Quine
    c. Leo Penn
    d. Daryl Duke

16. In 1997, <u>TV Guide</u> named "Murder by the Book" the 16th greatest television show of all time. It was directed by someone who would become one of Hollywood's most famous directors. Who is it?
   a. James Cameron
   b. Steven Spielberg
   c. George Lucas
   d. Ridley Scott

17. Leo Penn, Bernard L. Kowalski, and Vincent McEveety all directed episodes of COLUMBO. They also directed episodes of which one of these series?
   a. CANNON
   b. BARNABY JONES
   c. BARETTA
   d. DIAGNOSIS MURDER

18. Which directors or producers had progeny who acted on the show? (Choose all that apply.)
   a. Roland Kibbee
   b. Boris Sagal
   c. Patrick McGoohan
   d. Richard Irving
   e. Vincent McEveety
   f. Harvey Hart

19. Which director was killed in a tragic accident while filming a television mini-series?
   a. Bernard L. Kowalski
   b. Richard Quine
   c. Boris Sagal
   d. Alan J. Levi

20. True or False? Two of Patrick McGoohan's daughters are in episodes of COLUMBO.

QUIZ 2.3: The Writers (!!!)

1. Who has the most writing credits on COLUMBO?
   a. Peter S. Fischer
   b. Jackson Gillis
   c. Steven Bochco
   d. William Driskill

2. Who has the second-most writing credits?
   a. William Read Woodfield
   b. Steven Bochco
   c. Peter S. Fischer
   d. Larry Cohen

3. Which episode(s) did Peter Falk write?
   a. "Negative Reaction"
   b. "Playback"
   c. "Short Fuse"
   d. "It's All in the Game"

4. Which episode(s) did Patrick McGoohan write?
   a. "Ashes to Ashes"
   b. "Murder with Too Many Notes"
   c. "Agenda for Murder"
   d. "Identity Crisis"

5. Steven Bochco later became a household name for creating which television show(s)?
   a. L. A. LAW
   b. SIMON AND SIMON
   c. NYPD BLUE
   d. HILL STREET BLUES

6. "Double Exposure" was written by Stephen J. Cannell, who became one of television's most prolific creators and producers. Which show(s) did he create?
   a. THE GREATEST AMERICAN HERO
   b. THE ROCKFORD FILES
   c. HAWAII FIVE-O
   d. THE A-TEAM
   e. WISEGUY

7. Robert Van Scoyk won an Edgar Award from the Mystery Writers of America for writing the script for which episode?
   a. "Try and Catch Me"
   b. "Murder under Glass"
   c. "Make Me a Perfect Murder"
   d. "Lady in Waiting"

8. The only two episodes adapted from outside material were based on stories written by Ed McBain (aka Evan Hunter). Which ones were they?
   a. "Playback"
   b. "Last Salute to the Commodore"
   c. "No Time to Die"
   d. "Undercover"

9. Nearly all the genuine "whodunit"s were written by one person. Who was it?
   a. Steven Bochco
   b. James Frawley
   c. Stanley Ralph Ross
   d. Jackson Gillis

10. Which of these teleplays was/were written by Steven Bochco?* (Choose all that apply.)
    a. "Etude in Black"
    b. "Double Shock"
    c. "Murder by the Book"
    d. "Ransom for a Dead Man"
    e. "Lady in Waiting"

[*The story idea may have come from someone else.]

11. Which of these scripts was/were written by Peter Fischer?
    a. "By Dawn's Early Light"
    b. "Negative Reaction"
    c. "A Friend in Deed"
    d. "A Deadly State of Mind"
    e. "Publish or Perish"

12. Two COLUMBO writers and one writing team competed
    against each other at the 1972 Emmy Awards. Who were
    they?
    a. Jackson Gillis
    b. Steven Bochco
    c. Levinson and Link
    d. Dean Hargrove
    e. John T. Dugan

13. Who won?
    a. Jackson Gillis
    b. Steven Bochco
    c. Levinson and Link
    d. Dean Hargrove

14. Which writer was nominated twice?
    a. Peter S. Fischer
    b. Jeffrey Bloom
    c. Steven Bochco
    d. Howard Berk

15. Only one person wrote and directed the same episode.
    Who was it?
    a. Patrick McGoohan
    b. Peter Falk
    c. Robert Culp
    d. William Shatner

16. He wrote only two COLUMBO scripts, but one of these
    gentleman wrote 24 teleplays for MURDER, SHE WROTE.
    a. Jackson Gillis
    b. Robert van Scoyk
    c. Bill Driskill
    d. William Read Woodfield

17. Which writer acted in an episode that he wrote?
    a. Peter S. Feibleman
    b. Stanley Ralph Ross
    c. David Rayfiel
    d. Stephen J. Cannell

ANSWERS
QUIZ 2.1

1. False. They met at Elkins Park Junior High School in suburban Philadelphia, and became close friends quickly. Their writing partnership began in high school, where they collaborated on radio scripts, and saturnine short stories inspired by Poe and O. Henry.

2. False. They were directly involved only until the end of the first season. However, many of their story ideas were used after that, and they made themselves available, unofficially, as story consultants.

3. (a); 4. (c)

5. (d) Their biggest successes were MURDER, SHE WROTE (264 episodes); MANNIX (194 episodes); and COLUMBO (69 episodes) Although their involvement with COLUMBO ended after the first season, they were still credited as Executive Producers for the duration of the series.

6. True. Since this is a book about COLUMBO, there is a clue to the answer: the two writers are named Franklin and Ferris, which are alliterative, just like Levinson and Link. Please note the word "loosely." In the show, Franklin isn't talented, a trait shared by neither Levinson nor Link. However, Ferris is portrayed as a workaholic, a tendency of Levinson's which may have led to his death at age 52.

7. (a); 8. (b)

9. False. The exact opposite is the case. The guest actors and actresses admired Falk for his work ethic, and claimed that he elicited better performances from them. The producers, on the other hand, were impatient with him for causing them to miss deadlines and increase costs. Even so, they did praise him for his dedication to the role and devotion to the show.

10. (c)

11. All but (d)

12. (a)

13. (d) He was also nominated for THE BOB NEWHART SHOW.

QUIZ 2.2

1. (b) He directed 7 shows, all on ABC.

2. (a)

3. (b) He directed 6 episodes, followed by Patrick McGoohan, who directed 5. Kowalski and Hart both helmed 4. Levi and Richard Quine directed 3 each.

4. (d); 5. (c)

6. False. The opposite is true. They were angry that he insisted on doing it, because novices are seldom allowed to direct during the first season of a show, so they gave him the hardest one. He never again asked to direct.

7. (c) As of 2013, he is 98 years old, and still going strong.

8. (b), (d)

9. (a); 10. (a)

11. (b) He played Coach on CHEERS, but died after the third season, and was replaced by Woody Harrelson.

12. (d) Katey Sagal has a small part in "Candidate for Crime," which her father directed. She later starred in MARRIED WITH CHILDREN.

13. (c), (d), and (e) He directed all five, but he was not in the other two.

14. (a), (c)

15. (c) His children are musician and songwriter Michael Penn; actor Sean Penn, who was nominated for five Academy Awards, and won two; and actor Chris Penn (who is deceased).

16. (b); 17. (d)

18. (a), (b), (c) and (e) Vincent J. McEveety is in three shows. Jefferson Kibbee is in two. Katey Sagal and Catherine and Anne McGoohan are each in one.

19. (c) It happened when he was directing WORLD WAR III, a television miniseries, in Oregon in 1982. He turned the wrong way when exiting a helicopter and ran into the tail rotor.

20. True. Catherine is in "Ashes to Ashes." Her father is the funeral home director, and she is his assistant. Her younger sister, Anne, is in "Murder with Too Many Notes." A little nepotism never hurt anyone.

QUIZ 2.3

1. (b) He leads the pack with 11 writing credits.

2. (b) and (c) Both men wrote seven teleplays.

3. (d)

4. (a) and (b) He is not credited on "Ashes to Ashes," but IMDb.com recognizes him and Jeffrey Hatcher as the writers.

5. All except (b)

6. All except (c)

7. (b)

8. (c) and (d)

9. (d)

10. All except (d)

11. All except (a)

12. (a), (b) and (c)

13. (c) They won for "Death Lends a Hand."

14. (c) He didn't win either time.

15. (a) There were two: "Murder with Too Many Notes" and "Ashes to Ashes" (in which he also starred). Peter Falk wrote one episode ("It's All in the Game") and directed a different one ("Blueprint for Murder").

16. (b) Jackson Gillis also wrote two episodes of that series.

17. (a) The episode is "Old Fashioned Murder". He plays the doctor who is Janie Brandt's fiance and the brother of the security guard who is killed.

PART THREE

GUEST STARS

QUIZ 3.1: AMERICA'S MOST WANTED

QUIZ 3.2: STARS as VILLAINS
(Part 1)

QUIZ 3.3: STARS as VILLAINS
(Part 2)

QUIZ 3.4: STARS as VICTIMS

QUIZ 3.1: America's Most Wanted (!)

Here they are, folks! A rogues gallery of the worst offenders on COLUMBO. A mini crime wave. These five scofflaws all committed murder in more than one episode. (They must have been paroled after the first time for good behavior.) Three of the five did the heinous deed on both NBC and ABC.

(a) ROBERT CULP; (b) PATRICK McGOOHAN (c) JACK CASSIDY (d) WILLIAM SHATNER; (e) GEORGE HAMILTON

1. Who violates the Sixth Commandment in the most episodes?

2. Who commits the most murders? (Hopefully, the reader understands that I mean "fictional murders." I don't want to be sued for libel.)

3. What three-time murderer had a son who was a teen singing sensation and actor in the 1970s?

4. This actor is undoubtedly best known for his "star"ring role aboard a certain spaceship. In "Butterfly in Shades of Gray," he plays Fielding Chase, a pompous radio talk show host who is pathologically possessive of his grown foster daughter.

5. Who plays Ken Franklin, the less talented half of a mystery writing team, who kills his partner in "Murder by the Book"?

6. Which actor plays Dr. Bart Keppel, the arrogant media consultant who specializes in subliminal advertising, in "Double Exposure"?

7. Who plays Eric Prince, the mortician to the stars (and "Mortician of the Year") in "Ashes to Ashes"?

8. This exceedingly handsome actor never quite fulfilled his early promise, but he has acted in everything from serious biopics, to campy spoofs, to commercials, to a reality show. He even hosted his own talk show (with his then-wife). Besides his acting career, he is known (and probably envied) for his perpetual suntan, and for having dated Lynda Bird Johnson, the President's daughter.

9. Which actor is Canadian?

10. What repeat offender returned to the show in the last season to play the lawyer father of a college student accused of murder, in "Columbo Goes to College"? It is his only appearance, out of four, when he isn't a killer. (Maybe rehabilitation is possible, after all.)

11. Who plays Dr. Marcus Collier, a callous psychiatrist who hypnotizes his lover (and patient) into killing herself?

12. Who earned eight Emmy nominations?

13. In his second appearance on the show (on ABC), who plays Wade Anders, the host of "Crime Alert"?

14. Who plays Ward Fowler, an actor with a mild case of multiple personality disorder who kills his blackmailing ex-lover in "Fade in to Murder"?

15. Which actor wrote, directed and starred in the innovative (albeit short-lived) 1960s TV series THE PRISONER?

QUIZ 3.2: Stars as Villains
(Part 1)

COLUMBO fans are blessed that so many talented thespians volunteered to be murderers, victims and supporting players. Some of them were unknown at the time, but went on to greater success. Others had already enjoyed a long and distinguished career, and they appeared on the show as guest stars. With first-rate scripts, intriguing plots, and clever sleuthing, not to mention an engaging lead character, COLUMBO would likely have been a hit show even with lesser talents. But it didn't hurt to have the best in the business in front of the cameras.

1. This beautiful actress starred in several classic Westerns and two Hitchcock movies, plus THE TWILIGHT ZONE, THE OUTER LIMITS, and other television shows. She portrays an ambitious cosmetics queen who kills twice in "Lovely but Lethal."
    a. Vera Miles
    b. Janet Leigh
    c. Anne Baxter
    d. Kim Novak

2. This Shakespearean actor gives a dynamic performance as a motivational speaker and psychologist who has a passion for classic movies, and owns a pair of dogs that are trained to kill. Who is the charismatic killer in "How to Dial a Murder"?
    a. Albert Finney
    b. Nicol Williamson
    c. Richard Burton
    d. Richard Basehart

3. One killer, a decorated Marine Corps General, romances the young woman who witnessed his crime, in the hope of persuading her that what she saw was an illusion. Who plays this deceitful war hero, in "Dead Weight"?
    a. Patrick McGoohan
    b. Robert Culp
    c. Richard Basehart
    d. Eddie Albert

4. Who plays a proud retired matador named Luis Montoya, in "A Matter of Honor"? (He is probably best known for his starring role on a television series created by Aaron Spelling.)
   a. Pedro Armendariz, Jr.
   b. Ricardo Montalban
   c. Mel Ferrer
   d. A. Martinez

5. What famous country singer does a turn as a murderer in "Swan Song"?
   a. George Jones
   b. Willie Nelson
   c. Johnny Cash
   d. Hank Williams, Jr.

6. Who plays a ruthless and ambitious surgeon in "A Stitch in Crime"? (He was in a famous sci-fi television show.)
   a. Leonard Nimoy
   b. Patrick Bauchau
   c. Nehemiah Persoff
   d. Anthony Zerbe

7. In "Rest in Peace, Mrs. Columbo," this actress plays an obsessed real estate agent bent on revenge against Columbo, who sent her recently deceased husband to prison many years earlier.
   a. Lola Albright
   b. Deidre Hall
   c. Helen Shaver
   d. Jeannie Berlin

8. He was a child star, but he commits a very grown-up murder in "Candidate for Crime."
   a. Jackie Cooper
   b. Mickey Rooney
   c. Robert Blake
   d. Roddy McDowall

9. Respected both as an actor and a director, he was one of Peter Falk's closest friends. Who plays a brilliant, but philandering, orchestra conductor in "Etude in Black"?
   a. Ben Gazzara
   b. Louis Jourdan
   c. Anthony Andrews
   d. John Cassavetes

10. Known for his intensity, this actor plays a very sober wine connoisseur, and winery owner, who kills his playboy half-brother in "Any Old Port in a Storm."
    a. Anthony Zerbe
    b. Hector Elizondo
    c. Donald Pleasence
    d. Rod Steiger

11. This French actor plays a renowned, but crooked, restaurant critic in "Murder Under Glass." He kills a restaurant owner who is threatening to expose him.
    a. Maurice Chevalier
    b. Louis Jourdan
    c. Gerard Depardieu
    d. Charles Boyer

12. Who plays a Deputy Police Commissioner who kills his wife, in "A Friend in Need"?
    a. Richard Kiley
    b. Richard Anderson
    c. Theodore Bikel
    d. Leslie Nielsen

13. Which star(s) of the television show THE WILD WILD WEST appear(s) on COLUMBO?
    a. Robert Conrad
    b. Whitey Hughes
    c. Ross Martin
    d. Dick Cangey

14. Who won an Emmy for Best Lead Actress for her work on the show? (Choose all that apply.)
    a. Blythe Danner
    b. Tyne Daly
    c. Faye Dunaway
    d. Gena Rowlands
    e. Lee Grant

15. Siblings don't always fight. If there is a sizable inheri-
    tance involved, they can get along famously. Which
    former television spy plays a tag team of ruthless twin
    brothers in "Double Shock"?
    a. Robert Culp
    b. Robert Vaughn
    c. Martin Landau
    d. Peter Graves

16. Which future CHEERS star plays a killer who owns a
    thoroughbred breeding ranch, in "Strange Bedfellows"?
    a. Kelsey Grammer
    b. George Wendt
    c. Woody Harrelson
    d. John Ratzenberger

17. Which of these STAR TREK veterans did Columbo have to
    arrest? (Choose all that apply.)
    a. William Shatner
    b. Leonard Nimoy
    c. George Takei
    d. Walter Koenig
    e. James Doohan

18. Which of these former spies play(s) a killer on COLUMBO?
    a. David McCallum
    b. Martin Landau
    c. Robert Culp
    d. Robert Vaughn
    e. Peter Graves

19. Which of these Hitchcock heroines play killers?
    a. Vera Miles and Janet Leigh
    b. Janet Leigh and Ingrid Bergman
    c. Ingrid Bergman and Tippi Hedren
    d. Tippi Hedren and Eva Marie Saint

20. He won an Academy Award in 1945 for his gripping
    portrayal of an alcoholic, in THE LOST WEEKEND. In "The
    Greenhouse Jungle," he is an opportunistic killer with a
    love of orchids. Who is this urbane English gentleman?
    a. John Gielgud
    b. Ray Milland
    c. Wilfrid Hyde-White
    d. Alec Guinness

21. Best known for his role in a prime time soap opera, this actor plays Col. Frank Brailie, a weekend commando who turns killer in "Grand Deceptions."
    a. Mel Ferrer
    b. Patrick Duffy
    c. Robert Foxworth
    d. Larry Hagman

22. Which of these stars of famous Broadway musicals play(s) a killer?
    a. Richard Kiley – MAN OF LA MANCHA
    b. Janet Leigh – BYE BYE BIRDIE
    c. Theodore Bikel – FIDDLER ON THE ROOF
    d. Clive Revill – OLIVER!
    e. Howard Keel – OKLAHOMA!

QUIZ 3.3: Stars as Villains (!)
(Part 2)

(a) Robert Conrad / (b) Laurence Harvey / (c) Tyne Daly
(d) Hector Elizondo / (e) Jose Ferrer / (f) Ruth Gordon
(g) Joyce Van Patten / (h) Roddy McDowall / (i) Gene Barry
(j) Anne Baxter / (k) Faye Dunaway

NOTE: Names may be used twice, and all names are used.

1. She won an Oscar for Best Supporting Actress for the horror classic ROSEMARY'S BABY. Heartbroken over the death of her niece, she exacts bitter revenge in "Try and Catch Me."

2. Which murderer played an infamous outlaw in the (real-life) movies? She plays socialite Lauren Staton In "It's All in the Game," her only COLUMBO appearance.

3. She won an Oscar for Best Supporting Actress in THE RAZOR'S EDGE, and was Frank Lloyd Wright's granddaughter. She plays Nora Chandler, a has-been actress, in "Requiem for a Falling Star."

4. Only two guest actresses kill twice with premeditation. Name the actress whose murders are in the same scene. (She plays an "old maid" in the episode. The scene is the family-owned museum.)

5. Name the actress whose murders are in different scenes. (She plays the alcoholic wife of a millionaire football team owner.)

6. Which actor is perfectly suited to his role as a fitness guru and health club owner in "An Exercise in Fatality"?

7. Who was married to Rosemary Clooney? (For the benefit of younger readers, she was a singer/actress, and George Clooney's aunt.)

8. He has had numerous television and film roles over a career spanning 50 years. In "A Case of Immunity," he plays the ruthless First Secretary of the Legation of a fictional Middle Eastern country. Who is this versatile actor? (You may remember him from CHICAGO HOPE.)

9. He was nominated for three Academy Awards, winning one in 1950 for CYRANO DE BERGERAC. In "Mind Over Mayhem," he plays a father who kills in order to protect his son from a charge of plagiarism.

10. This Lithuanian-born British actor made a name for himself with ROOM AT THE TOP (for which he received an Oscar nomination), but he is probably best remembered for his role in THE MANCHURIAN CANDIDATE. In "The Most Dangerous Match," he plays a chess grandmaster who would rather commit murder than lose the world championship.

11. Despite a solid law enforcement background on television, including BAT MASTERSON and BURKE'S LAW, this debonair actor plays a shrink who can't resist doing away with his wife in "Prescription: Murder."

12. His acting career began at age 10 and continued until his death from cancer at age 70. His credits include BATMAN (on television), and both the movie and television versions of PLANET OF THE APES (and its sequels). In "Short Fuse," he plays a slightly crazed chemist and photography buff who refuses to let a blackmailer ruin his chance to inherit the company his late father founded.

13. Who was the oldest murderer on the show?
    a. Janet Leigh
    b. Ray Milland
    c. Ruth Gordon
    d. Eddie Albert

14. Who was the youngest murderer?
    a. Fisher Stevens
    b. Gary Hershberger
    c. Claudia Christian
    d. Steven Caffrey

QUIZ 3.4: Stars as Victims (!!)

In every murder there is a victim, of course. The victims on COLUMBO aren't quite as prominent as the murderers because, well, they're dead. They don't have much to do during the time that remains after the crime has been committed, which is most of the program. But quite a few famous names (or faces) have given their lives as martyrs to our entertainment. The least we can do is acknowledge their sacrifice, and give credit where it is due. All the names are used, and used only once.

(a) John Dehner / (b) Lola Albright / (c) Pat Crowley
(d) Rue McClanahan / (e) Richard Anderson / (f) Ida Lupino
(g) Bradford Dillman / (h) Lesley Ann Warren
(i) Jack Kruschen / (j) Lew Ayres / (k) Greg Evigan
(l) John Kerr / (m) Nina Foch (n) Martha Scott
(o) Steve Forrest / (p) Martin Milner / (q) Fionnula Flanagan
(r) Sal Mineo / (s) Anthony Zerbe / (t) Nehemiah Persoff

1. An actress since the early 1950s, she earned an Emmy nomination for PETER GUNN, her most enduring role. Who plays Clare Daley, Ward Fowler's ex-lover and blackmailer, in "Fade in to Murder"?

2. She has two stars on Hollywood's Walk of Fame – one for movies, and one for television – and she won an Emmy Award for LOU GRANT. Who is the first unfortunate victim on COLUMBO?

3. She is probably best known as the randy Blanche Devereaux on THE GOLDEN GIRLS, a role for which she received four Emmy nominations (winning one). Who plays Verity Chandler, the gossip reporter who tries to blackmail Eric Prince (and pays for it with her life) in "Ashes to Ashes"?

4. A rare recipient of both a Daytime and a Primetime Emmy Award, he had various roles on MURDER, SHE WROTE, and a recurring one on FALCON CREST. Who is the victim of his uncle's dastardly betrayal in "The Greenhouse Jungle"?

5. He was nominated twice for a Best Supporting Actor Oscar (for EXODUS and REBEL WITHOUT A CAUSE). He was also successful as a singer, with a couple of top 40 hits in 1957. Who is the second victim in "A Case of Immunity"?

6. This legendary actress was a true Hollywood "Renaissance woman." Besides acting, she directed television shows as early as 1950, when there were few other female directors. She also wrote scripts for both television and the movies. Who plays Tommy Brown's wife/victim, in "Swan Song"?

7. A Harvard graduate, he starred in 75 episodes of PEYTON PLACE, and the movie SOUTH PACIFIC. Who plays Col. Dutton, Maj. Gen. Hollister's victim in "Dead Weight"?

8. She was nominated for a Best Supporting Actress Oscar for VICTOR/VICTORIA, and starred in 23 episodes of MISSION: IMPOSSIBLE. Who falls victim to Dr. Mark Collier's treachery in "A Deadly State of Mind"?

9. He was a Disney animator and professional pianist before turning to acting in 1941. He had recurring roles on THE ROARING 20s, THE BAILEYS OF BALBOA (on which he played a Commodore) and, most notably, THE DORIS DAY SHOW. Who portrays Commodore Otis Swanson in "Last Salute to the Commodore"?

10. This Irish actress won an Emmy in 1976 for the mini-series RICH MAN, POOR MAN, and was a regular cast member on BROTHERHOOD. In "Murder: A Self Portrait," she plays the ex-wife of Max Barsini, who kills her because she knows a dark secret.

11. He was nominated for an Oscar in 1948 for JOHNNY BELINDA, and for an Emmy in 1972 for KUNG FU. Who plays the pipe-smoking Dr. Nicholson in "Mind Over Mayhem"?

12. An actor on both the big and small screens since the early 1950s, he is best known for two iconic television roles: Tod Stiles on ROUTE 66, and Officer Pete Malloy on ADAM-12. Who plays Jim Ferris, Ken Franklin's more talented writing partner in "Murder by the Book," whose very talent gets him killed?

13. This Jewish character actor has been in nearly 200 movies and television shows since 1948. Who plays the owner of the supper club whose star attraction is an ex-Nazi, in "Now You See Him…"?

14. She was nominated for an Oscar in 1940 for her first picture, OUR TOWN, playing the same character she had played on the stage. She played Dr. Hartley's mother on THE BOB NEWHART SHOW. Who plays Margaret Meadis, the doomed mother-in-law of the killer in "Playback"?

15. The winner of an Emmy Award in 1973 for HARRY O, this veteran actor is accustomed to playing villains. On COLUMBO, however, he is the victim. Who plays Max Dyson, the magician who loses his head in "Columbo Goes to the Guillotine"?

16. He is probably best known for his role as Oscar Goldman on THE SIX MILLION DOLLAR MAN and THE BIONIC WOMAN. Who plays Bryce Chadwick, the killer's controlling brother in "Lady in Waiting"?

17. He starred as Lt. Dan "Hondo" Harrelson on the television series S.W.A.T., and was a recurring character on DALLAS. In "A Bird in the Hand," he plays Big Fred McCain, the football team owner who is eliminated by his alcoholic, but ambitious, wife.

18. Prior to his appearance on COLUMBO, he was the star of two hit television series: B. J. AND THE BEAR, and MY TWO DADS. He plays the other victim of Dolores McCain, her gambling-addicted nephew Harold.

19. He has a small but memorable role as the bemused doctor in the movie THE APARTMENT. Who plays Tomlin Dudek, the chess-playing rival of the killer in "The Most Dangerous Match?"

20. She won a Golden Globe in 1954 for "Most Promising Female Newcomer." She starred as the harried wife and mother on television's PLEASE DON'T EAT THE DAISIES, and had recurring roles on DYNASTY and several sudsy dramas in the late 1980s and 1990s. Who plays Lenore Kennicut, the accidental victim in "Death Lends a Hand"?

ANSWERS
QUIZ 3.1

1. (b) He is the only one to satisfy his homicidal urges in four episodes. Culp and Cassidy play a murderer three times. Shatner and Hamilton play one twice.

2. (a), (b) and (c) are all guilty of 4 murders apiece. Hamilton kills a total of three people in two shows. Shatner kills one in each of two episodes.

3. (c) He died at the age of 49 in an apartment fire. His son is David Cassidy. After rocketing to fame as a singer, he was cast in THE PARTRIDGE FAMILY, on which he essentially played himself. It also starred his stepmother, Shirley Jones.

4. (d); 5. (c); 6. (a)

7. (b) Meaning no offense, he does look the part.

8. (e); 9. (d); 10. (a)

11. (e) The episode is "A Deadly State of Mind."

12. (b); 13. (e); 14. (d); 15. (b)

QUIZ 3.2

1. (a); 2. (b); 3. (d); 4. (b)

5. (c) An instance of art imitating life, although Cash was only convicted of manslaughter, unlike the show.

6. (a)

7. (c); 8. (a); 9. (d); 10. (c); 11. (b); 12. (a)

13. (a), (c) Both of them play murderers. Maybe upholding the law had gotten boring.

14. (c); 15. (c) 16. (b)

17. (a), (b). Walter Koenig is also on the show, but he doesn't play a killer.

18. (b), (c) and (d)

19. (a); 20. (b); 21. (c); 22. All except (e)

QUIZ 3.3

1. (f)

2. (k) In BONNIE AND CLYDE, her third movie, she plays Bonnie Parker, opposite Warren Beatty as Clyde Barrow.

3. (j) Although she didn't win an Academy Award for the role, she is probably best remembered for playing Eve Harrington, the upstart actress in the 1950 classic ALL ABOUT EVE.

4. (g) She is in two episodes. In the one where she isn't the killer, she plays a nun. (That's what I call <u>acting</u>.) Her older brother, Dick, played the father on EIGHT IS ENOUGH.

5. (c) She is also in two shows. In the other one, she plays an ex-hooker. (For a killer, not quite as much of a stretch as Van Patten's nun.) Although she didn't win an Emmy for COLUMBO, she racked up an unprecedented 17 nominations (six wins) for roles on CAGNEY AND LACEY, JUDGING AMY and CHRISTY. Her brother, Tim, is also an actor. He starred on the television show WINGS.

6. (a) He was in the television show THE WILD WILD WEST.

7. (e); 8. (d); 9. (e)

10. (b) He died at 45 of cancer, possibly induced by alcohol and drug abuse.

11. (i); 12. (h)

13. (c) She was 81 years old at the time.

14. (a) He was 25, younger than the college students who are killers in "Columbo Goes to College."

QUIZ 3.4

1. (b) She was in three television shows starring actors who play killers on COLUMBO: BURKE'S LAW (Gene Barry); THE DICK VAN DYKE SHOW; and THE MAN FROM U.N.C.L.E. (Robert Vaughn).

2. (m)

3. (d)

4. (g)

5. (r) He died tragically at age 37 in a mugging incident.

6. (f) She is also Roger Stanford's aunt in "Short Fuse."

7. (l)

8. (h)

9. (a) He also has a small part in "Swan Song."

10. (q)

11. (j) He has two stars on Hollywood's Walk of Fame: one for movies, and one for radio.

12. (p)

13. (t) When declining health forced him to cut back on acting work, he took up watercolor painting at 65, and is exhibited in galleries up and down the West Coast.

14. (n)

15. (s)

16. (e)

17. (o) He was the youngest of 13 children, one of whom was actor Dana Andrews. "Forrest" was actually his middle name.

18. (k)

19. (i)

20. (c)

PART FOUR

THE PLAYERS

QUIZ 4.1: UNSUNG HEROES

QUIZ 4.2: DOUBLE DUTY

QUIZ 4.3: OTHER GIGS

QUIZ 4.4: FUTURE STARS

QUIZ 4.1: Unsung Heroes (!!!)

COLUMBO is one of the few shows in the history of television to have no cast (besides the central figure), and no recurring characters (unless you count the raincoat and the car). It could even be unique that way, but since I am not an expert on the subject, I don't want to go out on a limb. The closest thing to a regular cast member is the Basset hound, and even he isn't in all the episodes. However, there are about a dozen performers who appear in at least two shows; the range of their talent is evident in the variety of the roles they play.   They always add texture to the show, and frequently humor, as well.

*CHOOSE ALL THAT APPLY.

1. John Finnegan plays which of these parts?*
   a. Lieutenant Duffy
   b. The assistant director of a TV show
   c. Police Chief Quentin Corbett
   d. A guard at a military base
   e. A bellhop

2. Which of these characters does Vito Scotti play?*
   a. Mr. Grindell, funeral director
   b. Mr. Chadwick, clothier
   c. An ice cream vendor
   d. A Maitre d' Hotel
   e. Vito, restaurant/bar owner

3. Which of these vocations does Shera Danese have?*
   a. The owner of an art gallery
   b. An associate in a law office
   c. The wife of a millionaire
   d. A fashion model
   e. The secretary to a television producer

4. Which of these roles does Shera Danese assume?*
   a. Killer
   b. Accessory (before the fact)
   c. Accomplice to murder
   d. Homicide victim

5. In what episode does she debut on COLUMBO?
   a. "Murder Under Glass"
   b. "Fade in to Murder"
   c. "Murder: A Self Portrait"
   d. "Old Fashioned Murder"

6. Which of these roles does Fred Draper play?*
   a. Thomas Dolan, in "Negative Reaction"
   b. Dr. Murchison, the chemist in "Lovely But Lethal"
   c. Swanny Swanson, in "Last Salute to the Commodore"
   d. David Morris, the blind "witness" in "A Deadly State of Mind"
   e. An anonymous cab driver in "Lady in Waiting"

7. Which role(s) does Val Avery play?*
   a. Artie Jessup, cat burglar – "A Friend in Deed"
   b. Ralph Dobbs, private eye – "The Most Crucial Game"
   c. Louie, the bartender – "Identity Crisis"
   d. Mr. Weekly, driver's license examiner – "Negative Reaction"

8. Rosanna Huffman plays an art student (and an accomplice) in "Suitable for Framing." She is a prospective home buyer in the opening scene of "Rest in Peace, Mrs. Columbo." But her most important role was off-camera. What was it?
   a. Set Decorator
   b. Costume Designer
   c. She was married to Richard Levinson.
   d. She was married to William Link.

9. True or False? None of the recurring actors and actresses is a victim.

10. True or False? None of the recurring players is a killer.

11. Which actor makes the most appearances (including minor roles)?
    a. Mike Lally
    b. John Finnegan
    c. Vito Scotti
    d. Fred Draper
    e. Val Avery

12. Which actress makes the most appearances (including minor roles)?
    a. Rosanna Huffman
    b. Shera Danese
    c. Sondra Currie
    d. Mariette Hartley
    e. Anne Francis

13. Which recurring character makes the most appearances?
    a. Sgt. George Kramer
    b. Barney, the restaurateur
    c. George, the Medical Examiner
    d. "Dog"

14. We never see Mrs. Columbo, but we see a lot of Mrs. Falk. Who is she?
    a. Shera Danese
    b. Rosanna Huffman
    c. Barbara Rhoades
    d. Sondra Currie

15. He is the closest Columbo ever comes to having a real "sidekick." Who plays Sergeant George Kramer, in six episodes?
    a. Bob Dishy
    b. Steven Gilborn
    c. Bruce Kirby
    d. John (J. P.) Finnegan

QUIZ 4.2: Double Duty (!)

The actors and actresses who appear on COLUMBO are not only talented, but also versatile. They might play a victim in one episode, and a suspect in another. Or they might play a killer each time, but with entirely different vocations. The following questions relate to these wearers of two or more hats.

(a) Tim O'Connor / (b) Dabney Coleman / (c) Joyce Van Patten
(d) Ed Begley, Jr. / (e) Leslie Nielsen / (f) Bernard Fox
(g) Patrick O'Neal / (h) Dean Stockwell / (i) Ray Milland
(j) Wilfrid Hyde-White / (k) Anne Francis / (l) Martin Landau
(m) Mariette Hartley / (n) Val Avery / (o) Deidre Hall

NOTE: Names are used only once, and all are used.

1. Who portrays a nun in "Negative Reaction," and Ruth Lytton (the murderer) in "Old Fashioned Murder"?

2. Who plays the killer in "Columbo and the Murder of a Rock Star," and Detective Murray in "Double Shock"?

3. Which actor plays twin brothers in the same episode (one or both of whom is/are guilty of the murder of their uncle)?

4. Which actor plays a murderer in "The Greenhouse Jungle," and the victim's husband in "Death Lends a Hand"?

5. Who is a lounge pianist (and suspect) in "Troubled Waters," and a lackadaisical football team owner (and victim) in "The Most Crucial Game"?

6. Who plays an architect (and killer) in "Blueprint for Murder," and an executive (a minor role) in "Make Me a Perfect Murder"?

7. Who plays Artie Jessup, cat burglar and suspect, in "A Friend in Deed," and Ralph Dobbs, private eye, in "The Most Crucial Game"?

8. Who is a ship's purser in "Troubled Waters," and a Chief of Detectives at New Scotland Yard in "Dagger of the Mind"?

9. Who has a small role as an animal control officer in "How to Dial a Murder," and plays a crooked insurance investigator (the killer) in "Undercover"?

10. Which actress plays a belly-dancing publisher's assistant in "Publish or Perish," and a personal secretary to the killer in "Try and Catch Me"?

11. Which actor plays a tight-fisted museum curator (and victim) in "Old Fashioned Murder," and a lawyer (and suspect) in "Double Shock"?

12. What superannuated actor plays a butler (and victim) in "Dagger of the Mind," and a lawyer in "Last Salute to the Commodore"?

13. This actress made a name for herself on DAYS OF OUR LIVES. She plays a victim in "Columbo Cries Wolf," and a receptionist in "Mind Over Mayhem."

14. What actor, known primarily for comedy roles, is a CIA operative (and victim) in "Identity Crisis," and a lawyer (and the fiance of the murderer) in "Lady in Waiting"?

15. What actress is a nurse (and victim) in "A Stitch in Crime," and the girlfriend of a crazy young chemist (the killer) in "Short Fuse"?

QUIZ 4.3: Other Gigs (!)

(a) Myrna Loy / (b) George Wendt / (c) Dean Jagger
(d) Anthony Andrews / (e) Lindsay Crouse / (f) Rip Torn
(g) William Windom / (h) James Read / (i) Patrick Macnee
(j) Ian Buchanan / (k) Julie Newmar / (l) Dabney Coleman
(m) Ed Begley, Jr. / (n) Honor Blackman / (o) Billy Connolly
(p) Barbara Colby / (q) Jessica Walter / (r) Don Ameche

1. She was Catwoman on the original BATMAN television
    series. In "Double Shock," she plays the victim's fiancee,
    who then becomes a victim herself. Who is she?

2. He is one of only two guest actors to receive an Emmy
    nomination for COLUMBO. Who plays the vindictive lawyer
    in "Columbo and the Murder of a Rock Star"?

3. He is from Scotland, and is known primarily as a comedian,
    not an actor. He plays Findlay Crawford, the envious com-
    poser in "Murder with Too Many Notes."

4. A regular cast member on REMINGTON STEELE, his break-
    through role was the lead (George Hazard) in the TV mini-
    series NORTH AND SOUTH. In "Uneasy Lies the Crown," he
    plays a gambling-addicted dentist who kills his wife's lover.

5. He has received acclaim for his work on the stage (a Tony
    nomination, and two Obie Awards) and on television (six
    consecutive Emmy nominations - one win - for "The Larry
    Sanders Show"). This Texas-born character actor is also a
    director. Who portrays the back-stabbing uncle in "Death
    Hits the Jackpot"?

6. The actress who plays Lily La Sanka in "Murder by the
    Book" died tragically at the age of 36 in a drive-by shoot-
    ing. Who was she?

7. He was born in London, and spent most of his early career
    on the stage in West End theaters. He made his mark on
    television (and earned an Emmy nomination) playing
    Sebastian Flyte in the mini-series BRIDESHEAD REVISITED
    in 1981. Who plays the vengeful "psychic" in "Columbo
    Goes to the Guillotine"?

8. She was born in New York City, and graduated from Rad-
   cliffe. She played a judge in both LAW AND ORDER and
   LAW AND ORDER: SPECIAL VICTIMS UNIT, but she is on
   the wrong side of the law this time. Who plays Dr. Joan
   Allenby, the sex therapist and killer in "Sex and the Married
   Detective"?

9. Like Billy Connolly, this guest star hails from Scotland. His
   good looks launched him on a career as a fashion model
   initially, but after a few years of jet-setting around the
   world, he became an actor. His first role was on "It's Garry
   Shandling's Show," which he was doing at the time of his
   COLUMBO appearance. He has starred in half a dozen soap
   operas, earning five Daytime Emmy nominations (one win)
   for THE BOLD AND THE BEAUTIFUL. Who plays Sean
   Brantley, the devious magazine publisher in "Columbo Cries
   Wolf"?

10. His father (after whom he is named) was a well-known
    actor who starred in TWELVE ANGRY MEN. He himself
    became recognizable to millions of television viewers from
    his role on the very popular ST. ELSEWHERE. He has a
    small part in "How to Dial a Murder." In his second
    appearance, he plays Irving Krutch, the crooked Prince-
    ton educated insurance investigator in "Undercover."

11. If the actor in the previous question is known to millions
    of television viewers, this one is probably known to a
    billion (almost). No matter what he does for the rest of
    his career, he will forever be "Norm" to everyone who
    watched CHEERS. In the tradition of Cain and Abel, he
    dispatches his brother to an early grave in "Strange Bed-
    fellows." Who plays the ruthless Graham McVeigh?

12. She has acted in numerous television series, including
    many detective shows. She starred as San Francisco's
    first female Chief of Detectives on AMY PRENTISS. In
    "Mind Over Mayhem," she plays the much younger
    psychologist wife of Dr. Nicholson, the victim.

13. In a career spanning almost 60 years, he was in dozens
    of television programs, most notably THE FARMER'S
    DAUGHTER and MURDER, SHE WROTE. He was also the
    prosecutor in TO KILL A MOCKINGBIRD. In "Short Fuse,"
    he plays Roger Stanford's nemesis, Everett Logan.

14. A star in the movies and on the radio since the 1940s, this handsome actor won an Oscar in 1986 for COCOON. Who plays Edna Matthews' lawyer in "Suitable for Framing"?

15. He played the always dapper John Steed on THE AVENGERS (1961-69). Who is the ship's captain in "Troubled Waters."?

16. She was James Bond's love interest in GOLDFINGER. In "Dagger of the Mind" she plays an actress who accidentally kills a theater producer during an argument.

17. What veteran character actor plays a lawyer in "The Most Crucial Game"? (He is probably best known for a classic Christmas movie.)

18. What famous fictional wife of a famous fictional detective guest stars as Alex Benedict's mother-in-law in "Etude in Black"?

QUIZ 4.4: Future Stars

In order to be a Guest Star, one has to be a Star first. All the performers who play villains on COLUMBO, and most of those who are victims, had already made their mark in Hollywood or on Broadway. This quiz focuses on the actors and actresses who would become bigger names after their appearance(s) on the show. All the names are used, and used only once.

(a) Suzanne Pleshette / (b) Will Geer / (c) Kim Cattrall
(d) Pat Harrington, Jr. / (e) Tyne Daly / (f) Vic Tayback
(g) Bruno Kirby / (h) Dean Stockwell/ (i) Jamie Lee Curtis
(j) Gwyneth Paltrow / (k) Pat Morita / (l) Sorrell Booke
(m) Valerie Harper / (n) Martin Sheen / (o) Mariette Hartley

1. This popular actor was well-known for "Happy Days," but he became a household name as Mr. Miyagi in four KARATE KID movies. He plays a butler in "Etude in Black."

2. In "How to Dial a Murder," this actress plays a house guest who is traumatized by the carnage left after two Doberman Pinschers attack an unsuspecting man in the kitchen. She became a megastar 20 years later on SEX AND THE CITY.

3. What future star of LAW AND ORDER: SPECIAL VICTIMS UNIT is in "Try and Catch Me" and "Publish or Perish"?

4. What future handyman on a long-running TV comedy show is in "An Exercise in Fatality"?

5. What future scream queen (on the big screen) broke into television playing a waitress with an attitude in "The Bye-Bye Sky High IQ Murder Case"?

6. Blythe Danner plays the wife of the killer (John Cassavetes) in "Etude in Black." At the time, Ms. Danner was pregnant with a daughter, who would become a famous actress herself. Who is she?

7. She plays call girl (and P. I. operative) Eve Babcock in "The Most Crucial Game." A few years later she had a starring role on THE MARY TYLER MOORE SHOW, which spun off into her own show.

8. Which future owner of a famous TV diner plays a rather surly avant-garde painter in "Suitable for Framing"?

9. The wife of a famous psychologist on another television series witnesses a murder in "Dead Weight." She plays an elementary school teacher in that episode.

10. What future DUKES OF HAZZARD star is a victim with an extremely high IQ?

11. What folksy veteran of movies and television plays a surgeon (who needs surgery) in "A Stitch in Crime"?

12. He falls victim to a heavy microscope wielded by a scorned woman in "Lovely but Lethal." Fifteen years later he found himself in the White House on a critically acclaimed series.

13. He plays a cadet at Haynes Military Academy in "By Dawn's Early Light" (his only episode). He would go on to star in many movies, including CITY SLICKERS and WHEN HARRY MET SALLY. His father was a COLUMBO regular, and co-stars in that show.

14. Who plays Dolores McCain, the killer in "A Bird in the Hand" and an ex-hooker in "Undercover"? A few years after being on COLUMBO, she went straight and became an Emmy Award-winning television detective herself.

15. He was hardly a new face, having appeared in numerous movies and television shows before COLUMBO. But his greatest success was still to come, as Scott Bakula's co-star on QUANTUM LEAP (1989-93). He plays a victim in "The Most Crucial Game," and an innocent suspect in "Troubled Waters."

ANSWERS

QUIZ 4.1

1. (e); 2. (c); 3. (d)

4. All but (a). She does everything but pull the trigger.

5. (b); 6. (a); 7. (d); 8. (c)

9. False. Shera Danese is a victim in "Undercover."

10. False. Fred Draper plays the killer in "Last Salute to the Commodore."

11. (a) Finnegan appears in 12, in many roles (one recurring). Kirby is in 9 episodes, playing different characters (one recurring). Scotti and Draper have six roles each.

12. (b) She is in six episodes, playing various parts. All the others are in two shows apiece.

13. (d) "Dog" is in nine shows; Sgt. Kramer, six; George, four; Barney, three.

14. (a)

15. (c) Oddly enough, after playing Sgt. Kramer six times, he returned in his last appearance ("Strange Bedfellows") to play a cop named Sgt. Phil Brindle. His son, Bruno, plays a cadet in "By Dawn's Early Light."

QUIZ 4.2

1. (c); 2. (b); 3. (l); 4. (i); 5. (h); 6. (g); 7. (n); 8. (f)

9. (d); 10. (m); 11. (a); 12. (j); 13. (o)

14. (e) He may be best known for his roles in AIRPLANE and the NAKED GUN movies.

15. (k) She played a detective herself on the short-lived TV show HONEY WEST.

QUIZ 4.3

1. (k); 2. (l); 3. (o); 4. (h); 5. (f); 6. (p)

7. (d); 8. (e); 9. (j); 10. (m); 11. (b)

12. (q); 13. (g); 14. (r); 15. (i); 16. (n)

17. (c) He played the retired General who owns the country inn in the film classic WHITE CHRISTMAS.

18. (a) She was Nora Charles, the wife of detective Nick Charles, in THE THIN MAN movies.

QUIZ 4.4

1. (k); 2. (c); 3. (o); 4. (d); 5. (i)

6. (j) She won an Academy Award for SHAKESPEARE IN LOVE.

7. (m)

8. (f) He played the owner of the diner on ALICE, and had the same role in ALICE DOESN'T LIVE HERE ANYMORE, the movie which inspired it.

9. (a) On THE BOB NEWHART SHOW, she played Dr. Bob Hartley's wife, Emily, who is also a teacher.

10. (l) This is ironic, but the irony is in reverse. He was a Yale graduate who spoke five languages.

11. (b) He is probably best known for his role as Zeb, the grandfather on THE WALTONS.

12. (n); 13. (g); 14. (e); 15. (h)

A REPLY TO CRITICS

With success inevitably comes criticism. COLUMBO received mostly praise, but there were a few critics who complained that it was "formulaic." They were right, but the criticism isn't valid. The show is formulaic in the same way that Shakespeare's sonnets, Monet's landscapes, and Bach's fugues are. All of them adhere to a recognizable form, but there is ample room for creativity within those parameters. Furthermore, the distinctive form is what enables observers, readers, and listeners to identify the creations of a particular artist, writer or composer. The form can become hackneyed or boring if the content is stale, but that was seldom the case with COLUMBO.

PART FIVE

THE CHARACTERS

QUIZ 5.1: RELATIONSHIPS

QUIZ 5.2: OCCUPATIONS
(NBC Episodes)

QUIZ 5.3: OCCUPATIONS
(ABC Episodes)

QUIZ 5.1: Relationships (!)

In both life and art, murderers and their victims are usually acquainted, and are even, in most cases, related. (Think about that the next time you worry about the rising crime rate.) In this quiz, you are asked to identify the relationship between the characters. (They are not always murderer and victim.)

1. How are Ken Franklin (killer) and Jim Ferris (victim) connected, in "Murder by the Book"?
   a. They are business partners.
   b. They are writing partners.
   c. Ferris is an attorney, and Franklin is his client.
   d. They are in love with the same woman.

2. What is the connection between General Hollister (killer) and Helen Stewart (witness), in "Dead Weight"?
   a. She is his niece.
   b. She is a secretary, and he is her boss.
   c. They are neighbors, but don't know each other.
   d. They are close friends.

3. In "Old Fashioned Murder," how are Ruth Lytton (killer) and Edward Lytton (victim) related?
   a. Husband and wife
   b. Father and daughter
   c. Cousins
   d. Brother and sister

4. What connects Dr. Barry Mayfield (murderer) and Sharon Martin (victim), in "A Stitch in Crime"? (Choose all that apply.)
   a. She is his nurse.
   b. She is his cleaning lady.
   c. She witnesses a dangerous and deceptive surgery he performs.
   d. She is his mistress.

5. Avaricious art critic Dale Kingston kills Rudy Matthews in "Suitable for Framing." What is their relationship?
   a. Father and son
   b. Romantic rivals
   c. Business partners
   d. Uncle and nephew

6. In "Double Shock," what is Clifford Paris (victim), to Norman and Dexter Paris (at least one of whom is the killer)?
   a. Their grandfather
   b. Their uncle
   c. Their brother
   d. Their father

7. In "The Bye-Bye Sky High IQ Murder Case," Oliver Brandt kills Bertie Hastings. How are they associated?
   a. They are friends, and partners in an accounting firm.
   b. They are co-owners of a chemical factory.
   c. They are President and Vice-President of a bank.
   d. They teach at the same high school.

8. What connects Emmett Clayton (killer) and Tomlin Dudek (victim) in "The Most Dangerous Match"?
   a. Dudek is a chess grandmaster, and Clayton is his manager.
   b. Clayton is a grandmaster, and Dudek is his manager.
   c. They are both grandmasters, and rivals.
   d. Clayton is a grandmaster, and Dudek is blackmailing him.

9. What is Ruth Lytton (killer), to Janie Brandt (suspect), in "Old Fashioned Murder"?
   a. Her aunt
   b. Her mother
   c. Her sister
   d. Her cousin

10. What is the relationship between Adrian Carsini (killer) and Ric Carsini (victim) in "Any Old Port in a Storm"?
   a. Brothers
   b. Half-brothers
   c. First cousins
   d. Second cousins

11. In "The Greenhouse Jungle," how is Jarvis Goodland (killer) related to Tony Goodland (victim)?
    a. Grandfather and grandson
    b. Father and son
    c. Uncle and nephew
    d. Brothers

12. How are Nora Chandler (killer) and Jean Davis (victim) connected, in "Requiem for a Falling Star"?
    a. Davis is Chandler's personal assistant.
    b. Davis is Chandler's dresser (she is an actress).
    c. Davis is Chandler's romantic rival.
    d. Davis is Chandler's press agent.

13. What is the connection between Viveca Scott (killer) and Karl Lessing (victim) in "Lovely but Lethal"?
    a. They are former lovers.
    b. He is a former employee of hers.
    c. He is her accountant.
    d. He is the owner of a rival cosmetics company.
    e. Both (a) and (b)

14. In "Publish or Perish," what is the association between Riley Greenleaf (killer) and Alan Mallory (victim)?
    a. They are writing partners.
    b. Greenleaf is Mallory's publisher.
    c. They are tennis partners at a country club.
    d. Mallory is Greenleaf's accountant.

15. In "A Friend in Deed," how are Columbo and Mark Halperin, the murderer, connected? (Choose all that apply.)
    a. They are neighbors.
    b. Halperin is Columbo's boss.
    c. Halperin once worked for Columbo's father.
    d. Halperin is a fellow cop.

16. What is the relationship between Edna Brown (victim) and Tommy Brown (killer), in "Swan Song"?
    a. Brother and sister
    b. Father and daughter
    c. First cousins
    d. Husband and wife

17. In "Troubled Waters," what is the connection between Hayden Danziger (killer) and Rosanna Wells (victim)?
    a. Wells is Danziger's mistress.
    b. Wells is Danziger's ex-wife.
    c. Wells is a singer in the lounge onboard ship.
    d. Wells is his secretary.
    e. Both (a) and (c)

18. What connects Margaret Midas (victim), and Harold Van Wick (killer), in "Playback"?
    a. They are neighbors.
    b. She is his sister-in-law.
    c. She is his mother-in-law.
    d. She owns the electronics company he works for.
    e. Both (c) and (d)

19. How are Henry Willis (victim) and actress Grace Wheeler (killer) related, in "Forgotten Lady"?
    a. He is her former manager.
    b. He is her current manager.
    c. They are husband and wife.
    d. He owns the movie studio where she is under contract.

20. What is the relationship between Dolores McCain and Harold McCain, in "A Bird in the Hand"?
    a. Brother and sister
    b. Husband and wife
    c. They are lovers.
    d. Aunt and nephew
    e. Both (c) and (d)

Gainful Employment

The villains in COLUMBO are the cream of society: educated, wealthy and powerful (not all three in every case, but at least two). Scanning the lists of vocations, one can't help but be impressed with the variety. The phrase "from every walk of life" might even suggest itself, except that there are no bricklayers, short order cooks, janitors, ditch diggers or factory workers. No, these are all professional people, which makes their involvement in the sordid business of homicide all the more intriguing.

Levinson and Link claimed that they got the ideas for most of the occupations from the Yellow Pages.

The next two quizzes ask you to match these high achievers with their occupations. All occupations are used. QUIZ 5.2 covers only the NBC episodes; QUIZ 5.3 relates to the ABC shows.

QUIZ 5.2: OCCUPATIONS
(NBC Episodes)

CHARACTERS

1. MARK HALPERIN (Richard Kiley)
2. ABIGAIL MITCHELL (Ruth Gordon)
3. HASSAN SALAH (Hector Elizondo)
4. KAY FREESTONE (Trish Van Devere)
5. DR. MARSHALL CAHILL (Jose Ferrer)
6. COLONEL LYLE C. RUMFORD (Patrick McGoohan)
7. MILO JANUS (Robert Conrad)
8. PAUL GALESKO (Dick Van Dyke)
9. DR. MARK COLLIER (George Hamilton)
10. HAYDEN DANZIGER (Robert Vaughn)
11. NORMAN PARIS (Martin Landau)
12. NELSON BRENNER (Patrick McGoohan)
13. WARD FOWLER (William Shatner)
14. OLIVER BRANDT (Theodore Bikel)
15. PAUL GERARD (Louis Jourdan)
16. LUIS MONTOYA (Ricardo Montalban)
17. DEXTER PARIS (Martin Landau)
18. TOMMY BROWN (Johnny Cash)
19. DR. BART KEPPEL (Robert Culp)
20. NELSON HAYWARD (Jackie Cooper)

OCCUPATIONS

(a) Celebrity chef

(b) CIA operative

(c) Military academy headmaster

(d) Retired matador and bull breeder

(e) Pulitzer Prize winning photographer

(f) Television executive

(g) Mystery writer

(h) Owner of a chain of fitness clubs

(i) Psychiatrist

(j) Head of a "think tank"

(k) Embassy attache

(l) Advertising psychologist

(m) Owner of a chain of used car dealerships

(n) Restaurant critic

(o) Certified Public Accountant

(p) Senatorial candidate

(q) Actor

(r) Banker

(s) Deputy police commissioner

(t) Gospel singer

QUIZ 5.3: OCCUPATIONS (!)
(ABC Episodes)

CHARACTERS

1. WAYNE JENNINGS (Andrew Stevens)

2. SEAN BRANTLEY (Ian Buchanan)

3. MAX BARSINI (Patrick Bauchau)

4. ELLIOTT BLAKE (Anthony Andrews)

5. DR. WESLEY CORMAN (James Read)

6. WADE ANDERS (George Hamilton)

7. LEON LAMARR (Rip Torn)

8. HUGH CREIGHTON (Dabney Coleman)

9. FIELDING CHASE (William Shatner)

10. IRVING KRUTCH (Ed Begley, Jr.)

OCCUPATIONS

(a) Beverly Hills jeweler

(b) Radio talk show host

(c) Tennis bum and playboy

(d) Defense attorney

(e) Painter

(f) Magazine publisher

(g) Celebrity dentist

(h) "CrimeAlert" television show host

(i) Insurance investigator

(j) Psychic

ANSWERS
QUIZ 5.1

1. (b); 2. (c); 3. (d); 4. (e)
5. (d); 6. (b); 7. (a); 8. (c)
9. (a); 10. (b); 11. (c); 12. (a)
13. (e); 14. (b); 15. (b); 16. (d)
17. (e); 18. (e); 19. (c)
20. (e) Yuck!

QUIZ 5.2

1. (s); 2. (g); 3. (k); 4. (f)
5. (j); 6. (c); 7. (h); 8. (e)
9. (i); 10. (m); 11. (r); 12. (b)
13. (q); 14. (o); 15. (n); 16. (d)
17. (a); 18. (t); 19. (l); 20. (p)

QUIZ 5.3

1. (c); 2. (f); 3. (e); 4. (j); 5. (g)
6. (h); 7. (a); 8. (d); 9. (b); 10. (i)

PART SIX

POLICE BLOTTER

QUIZ 6.1: JUST the FACTS, MA'AM

QUIZ 6.2: The PLOTS

QUIZ 6.3: SO CLOSE...
(NBC Episodes)

QUIZ 6.4: SO CLOSE...
(ABC Episodes)

QUIZ 6.1: Just the Facts, Ma'am
(!!!)

The title of this quiz is a quote, but not from Columbo. It was a favorite expression of Sgt. Joe Friday, the no-nonsense police detective on DRAGNET, which preceded COLUMBO.

1. Excluding accomplices and accessories, how many murderers are there on COLUMBO?
   a. 68
   b. 71
   c. 75
   d. 82

2. How many are women?
   a. 10
   b. 14
   c. 17
   d. 25

3. How many total murders are committed?
   a. 69
   b. 75
   c. 83
   d. 89

4. How many are involuntary manslaughter (true accidents)?
   a. None
   b. 2
   c. 4
   d. 6

5. How many are second-degree murder (not planned, but committed in anger)?
   a. 5
   b. 6
   c. 7
   d. 10

6. How many episodes have two murders?
   a. 11
   b. 14
   c. 19
   d. 22

7. How many have three or more murders?
   a. None
   b. 1
   c. 2
   d. 4

8. How many have two murderers who kill different people?
   a. 2
   b. 3
   c. 4
   d. 6

9. How many victims are killed because they know about the first murder (or attempted murder) in the show? They may be an accomplice, an accessory, a witness, or simply have deduced who the killer is. (Do not include those who know about a murder committed in the distant past.)
   a. 7
   b. 9
   c. 12
   d. 15

10. How many episodes involve a conspiracy? (One partici-pant is the killer; the other is either an accomplice or an accessory before the fact. Do not count cases where the accomplice isn't aware that murder is part of the deal.)
    a. 3
    b. 5
    c. 7
    d. 10

QUIZ 6.2: The Plots (!!)

1. In four episodes, Columbo is roped into an investigation when he is otherwise engaged (e.g. on a trip):

   A. In which one is he on a cruise?
   B. In which one is he in Tijuana, Mexico?
   C. In which one is he given a tour of Scotland Yard?
   D. In which one is he attending a wedding?

2. True or False? All of Columbo's suspects are brought to justice.

3. What is the only episode where Columbo does not meet the criminal?
   a. "No Time to Die"
   b. "Forgotten Lady"
   c. "Double Exposure"
   d. "Candidate for Crime"

4. True or False? Every COLUMBO episode involves a murder.

5. Which of these episodes is/are (a) "whodunit(s)"?
   a. "Last Salute to the Commodore"
   b. "Double Shock"
   c. "A Bird in the Hand"
   d. "Lovely but Lethal"
   e. "Undercover"

6. Which episode was filmed partly in London?
   a. "Dagger of the Mind"
   b. "Butterfly in Shades of Gray"
   c. "Publish or Perish"
   d. "Now You See Him..."

7. Which one of these episodes begins with involuntary manslaughter, but is followed by a first-degree murder?
   a. "Columbo Likes the Nightlife"
   b. "Grand Deceptions"
   c. "Negative Reaction"
   d. "Double Shock"

8. Which of these episode(s) begin(s) with a second-degree murder, but is followed by a first-degree murder?
   a. "Dagger of the Mind"
   b. "Death Lends a Hand"
   c. "A Friend in Deed"
   d. "Lovely but Lethal"

9. In "A Friend in Deed," how does Police Commissioner Mark Halperin compel his friend Hugh Caldwell to become an accessory in the murder of Mrs. Halperin?
   a. Halperin knows about an affair Caldwell is having.
   b. Halperin knows that Caldwell cheats on his taxes.
   c. Caldwell owes him $10,000 in poker losses, and he has agreed to forgive the debt, in exchange for his complicity.
   d. Caldwell killed his wife in an argument, and Halperin helped him cover it up.

10. Why is Adrian Carsini, in "Any Old Port in a Storm," so willing to let Columbo arrest him?

11. Graham McVeigh is even more eager to go with Columbo, in "Strange Bedfellows." What is his reason?

12. In "A Case of Immunity," Columbo has no authority to arrest the guilty party. But Hassan Salah practically begs Columbo to put the handcuffs on him. Why?

13. In what way is "Dagger of the Mind" a twist on MACBETH?

14. In which episode is Columbo accused of stealing another airplane passenger's luggage?
   a. "Dagger of the Mind"
   b. "Troubled Waters"
   c. "Lovely but Lethal"
   d. "An Exercise in Fatality"

15. The killer on an NBC show is named Carsini, and one on an ABC show is named Barsini. Their names differ by only one letter, and the murders are strikingly similar. In both cases, the homicide is made to look like what?
   a. A heart attack
   b. An accidental drowning
   c. A botched robbery
   d. A suicide

16. Which episode(s) feature(s) a policeman who is the killer?
    a. "A Trace of Murder"
    b. "Dead Weight"
    c. "Short Fuse"
    d. "A Friend in Deed"
    e. "Grand Deceptions"

17. In which episode(s) does the killer think his victim is
    dead, only to find out that he or she was only badly
    injured? (In one case, the victim does die later. In the
    other, the killer has to try something else, which succeeds
    that time.)
    a. "Try and Catch Me"
    b. "Prescription: Murder"
    c. "The Most Dangerous Match"
    d. "The Most Crucial Game"

18. In which episode(s) is Columbo assigned to a protection
    detail? (This would never happen in real life. Homicide
    detectives are too busy for routine jobs like that.
    Besides, Columbo doesn't know how to shoot.)
    a. "Candidate for Crime"
    b. "Agenda for Murder"
    c. "A Case of Immunity"
    d. "Identity Crisis"

19. In which episode(s) does a videotape (or film) resurface
    after many years and threaten to damage or destroy
    someone's reputation, which leads to the homicide?
    a. "Caution: Murder Can Be Hazardous to Your Health"
    b. "Murder, Smoke and Shadows"
    c. "An Exercise in Fatality"
    d. "Dead Weight"

20. In which episodes does someone who knows about the
    first murder try to extort the killer for something besides
    money (e.g. a job, romance)? The person is not neces-
    sarily killed.
    a. "Dagger of the Mind"
    b. "Any Old Port in a Storm"
    c. "Columbo and the Murder of a Rock Star"
    d. "Murder by the Book"

QUIZ 6.3: SO CLOSE... (!!)
(NBC Episodes)

These omissions, oversights, and missteps are not the only clues that bring down the killer, but in many cases they are what cause Columbo to suspect him or her in the first place, or they are the final nail in the coffin. The choices are listed after the questions. All the names are used. Long blanks take both a first and last name. Short blanks are only a first name.

1. If only _____ had remembered to turn the radio back to a country station, he would be a free man.

2. If (A)_____ hadn't written down the plot idea (B)_____ told him. . .

3. If (A)_____ had known that (B)_____'s contact lenses were both in place. . .

4. If _____ hadn't picked up the wrong umbrella. . .

5. If (A)_____'s nephew-in-law, (B)_____, hadn't had any matches. . .

6. If _____ hadn't left his party invitation in the living room, where it could be seen on the tape. . .

7. If _____ had remembered that the button on the other phone lights up when the extension is used. . .

8. If _____ had left the lights on. . .

9. If _____'s flower hadn't fallen out of his lapel button. . .

10. If (A)_____ had known her brother (B)_____ had a spare key hidden in the flowerpot. . .

11. If it <u>hadn't</u> rained while _____ was away in New York. . .

12. If it <u>had</u> rained at _____'s country estate. . .

13. If (A)_____ had known there was a drunk in the auto junkyard when he shot (B)_____. . .

14. If _____ had known that the projectionist always puts a nickel at the end of a reel of film. . .

15. If _____ hadn't mentioned in his speech that the Chinese withdrew from the Olympics. . .

16. If (A)_____ had only known that (B)_____ wore contact lenses. . .

CHOICES

(a) Brimmer

(b) Hassan Salah

(c) Alex Benedict

(d) Bryce

(e) Abigail Mitchell

(f) Nelson Brenner

(g) Beth Chadwick

(h) Nelson Hayward

(i) Rachman Habib

(j) Jim Ferris

(k) Harold Van Wick

(l) Elliot Markham

(m) Edmund

(n) Paul Galesko

(o) Dr. Bart Keppel

(p) Ken Franklin

(q) Nicholas Frame

(r) Lenore

(s) Alvin Deschler

(t) Sir Roger Haversham

(u) Ruth Lytton

(v) Adrian Carsini

QUIZ 6.4: SO CLOSE... (!!)
(ABC Episodes)

These omissions, oversights, and missteps are not the only clues that bring down the killer, but in many cases they are what cause Columbo to suspect him or her in the first place, or they are the final nail in the coffin. The choices are listed after the questions. All names are used (one twice). Long blanks take a first and last name; short blanks, only a first name.

1. If (A)_____ had noticed the envelope of money in (B)_____'s pocket. . .

2. If (A)_____ had known that (B)_____ had just faxed a joke to his wife. . .

3. If (A)_____ had noticed that (B)_____'s keys were missing from his pockets. . .

4. If (A)_____ had known a little more about women's panties, and (B)____had known a little less about them. . .

5. If (A)_____ had known that (B)____ got a haircut. . .

6. If _____ had put more fish in the middle tank at the rave club. . .

7. If _____ had known that two-star champagne has two stars on the cork. . .

8. If (A)_____ had remembered to have (B)____ wear (C)____'s beeper bracelet. . .

9. If (A)_____ had known that (B)_____'s watch was counterfeit. . .

10. If only the weather hadn't turned cold unexpectedly, and _____ hadn't turned up the thermostat. . .

11. If the hedges in front of _____'s office hadn't been trimmed. . .

12. If _____ hadn't taken a bite of cheese at the crime scene. . .

<u>CHOICES</u>

(a) Wayne Jennings

(b) Vivian Dimitri

(c) Oscar Finch

(d) Dolores McCain

(e) Sean Brantley

(f) Freddy

(g) Dr. Joan Allenby

(h) Lauren Staton

(i) Leon Lamarr

(j) Justin Price

(k) Harold

(l) Charlie Chambers

(m) Columbo

(n) Dian

(o) David Kincaid

(p) Tina

(q) Frank Staplin

(r) Wade Anders

(s) Hugh Creighton

ANSWERS
QUIZ 6.1

1. (c)

2. (b) Two of them kill accidentally, leaving only 12 who are guilty of premeditation. Three others are accomplices, and three more are accessories after the fact. Still, women apparently <u>are</u> the gentler sex.

3. (d)

4. (b) "A Bird in the Hand" (the gardener), and "Columbo Likes the Nightlife" (Tony Galper)

5. (a); 6. (c)

7. (b) "A Bird in the Hand" is the only one. The gardener is the third victim. The poor fellow was just in the wrong place at the wrong time.

8. (c); 9. (c); 10. (b)

QUIZ 6.2

1A. "Troubled Waters"

1B. "A Matter of Honor"

1C. "Dagger of the Mind"

1D. "No Time to Die"

2. False. Columbo does not arrest Grace Wheeler in "Forgotten Lady," for two reasons: 1. She is dying, and 2. She has Alzheimer's Disease, so she isn't even aware of what she did. He also doesn't arrest Lisa Martin in "It's All in the Game." She is only an accomplice, but she should still be prosecuted.

3. (a)

4. False. "No Time to Die" is about a kidnapping.

5. All except (d)

6. (a)

7. (a) The first murder is one of only two truly accidental deaths in the series. Vanessa kills her ex-husband when she pushes him away from her and he hits his head on a glass coffee table. It was self-defense, unlike the similar incident in "Death Lends a Hand," where Brimmer strikes his victim before she lands on the coffee table.

8. All but (b). None of the first murders are premeditated, but three of them are followed by a planned one. The second one in (a) and (d) is committed to silence someone who knows about the first one. The second one in (c) is committed by someone else.

9. (d)

10. The alternative is to marry his secretary, whom he calls an "Iron Maiden."

11. In his case, Vincent Fortelli, a Mafioso, is waiting to avenge the death of a friend whom McVeigh killed.

12. He is an Legation attache, with diplomatic immunity. But the King has arrived from his fictitious country to take him back home, where he will face Middle Eastern justice.

13. In Shakespeare's play, the wife (Lady Macbeth) goes crazy; in "Dagger of the Mind," the husband does.

14. (a); 15. (b)

16. (a) and (d)

17. (b) and (c)

18. (a) and (c)

19. (a) and (b)

20. All of them. In (a) the extortionist wants a job, which he gets, but is killed. In (b) she wants marriage, which she doesn't get, but isn't killed. In (c) she wants a job and marriage, both of which she gets, and isn't killed. In (d) she wants a romance, which she doesn't get, and is killed.

QUIZ 6.3

1. (l)

2A. (j), 2B. (p)

3A. (a), 3B. (r)

4. (q)

5A. (e), 5B. (m)

6. (k); 7. (h); 8. (u); 9. (c)

10A. (g), 10B. (d)

11. (v); 12. (t)

13A. (n), 13B. (s)

14. (o); 15. (f)

16A. (b), 16B. (i)

QUIZ 6.4

1A. (b), 1B. (l)

2A. (c), 2B. (q)

3A. (g), 3B. (o)

4A. (a), 4B. (m)

5A. (d), 5B. (k)

6. (j); 7. (s)

8A. (e), 8B. (p), 8C. (n)

9A. (i), 9B. (f)

10. (h); 11. (r); 12. (c)

PART SEVEN

THE CRIMES

QUIZ 7.1: MOTIVES (Part 1)

QUIZ 7.2: MOTIVES (Part 2)

QUIZ 7.3: MEANS

THE CRIMES

Most people, and certainly all armchair detectives who like mysteries, know that Motive, Means, and Opportunity are the unholy trinity of homicide. They are the essential components, just as heat, oxygen and fuel are the basic ingredients of fire. If any one of them is absent, the effect that is produced when all three are present will not result.

Motive is really the most interesting (to me, at any rate), so there are four quizzes on it. With the exception of a few sociopathic killers whose only purpose is to cause as much pain and suffering as possible, motive is the sine qua non of any homicide. In philosophical terms, it is both the first cause (it gets the ball rolling) and the final cause (it is the purpose of the act). It can also determine the punishment for the crime, if the legal system gets involved.

The Means (or Method) can be interesting if an unusual weapon is used, or if some kind of trickery is involved.

There is little to say about Opportunity, so there isn't a quiz on the subject. But there is a lot to say about the lack of Opportunity, which brings us to fake alibis, and there is a quiz on them in PART SEVEN, which deals with Deceptions.

QUIZ 7.1: MOTIVES (Part 1) (!)

"WHO KNOWS WHAT EVIL LURKS IN THE HEARTS OF MEN?"

The motives on COLUMBO range from the cold-blooded to the sympathetic. This is the first of four quizzes about what drives the killer to do what he or she does. All the titles are used, and they may be used more than once.

NBC EPISODES

(a) "The Greenhouse Jungle"

(b) "The Bye-Bye Sky High IQ Murder Case"

(c) "Lovely but Lethal"

(d) "Murder by the Book"

(e) "Requiem for a Falling Star"

(f) "Any Old Port in a Storm"

(g) "Old Fashioned Murder"

(h) "Suitable for Framing"

(i) "Death Lends a Hand"

(j) "A Stitch in Crime"

(k) "A Deadly State of Mind"

(l) "Ransom for a Dead Man"

(m) "By Dawn's Early Light"

(n) "Double Shock"

ABC EPISODES

(o) "Dagger of the Mind"

(p) "Death Hits the Jackpot"

(q) "Butterfly in Shades of Gray"

(r) "Murder with Too Many Notes"

(s) "Sex and the Married Detective"

1. In many episodes there are two murders, but in four of those listed here there is no motive for the first one, because it is a spontaneous act. It is committed in anger, so there is a degree of responsibility, but there is no "malice aforethought." Which of these shows depict(s) a second-degree murder?

2. The no-nonsense headmaster of the prestigious Haynes Military Academy so hates the idea of his beloved school becoming coeducational that he would rather see the founder's son killed than let that happen.

3. Ruth Lytton is a plain, middle-aged woman, and a spinster. She has no life outside the Lytton Museum. But her brother does not share her love of antiquities. He thinks the museum is a white elephant, and is planning to sell it. Ruth is driven by desperation to kill him. (Miss Lytton may be sympathetic, and so is her motive, but her willingness to frame her niece is not.)

4. Fielding Chase, radio talk show host, is a blowhard and a control freak. He has many enemies, but few friends. His only close relationship is with his foster daughter, the child of a woman he once loved, who died when the girl was in her early teens. He raised her as his own, but now she wants to pursue a career in New York as a writer. A male friend of hers, one of Chase's own employees, is encouraging her in this ambition. Chase believes that if he can only get him out of the way, his daughter would lose interest in the idea, and stay at home.

5. Dr. Barry Mayfield is a brilliant cardiac surgeon who has developed an anti-rejection drug for transplant patients that he is eager to tell the world about (not for altruistic reasons). But the head of the laboratory, Dr. Edmund Hidemann, feels that more testing is indicated before they go public. When Dr. Hidemann becomes ill and has to have a heart valve replaced, the impatient Dr. Mayfield sees an opportunity to get Dr. Hiedemann out of his way, by sabotaging the surgery. However, thanks to Columbo's timely intervention, he doesn't succeed. (Although Dr. Hidemann isn't killed, Columbo is involved because a nurse who participates in the surgery is.)

6. To say that Adrian Carsini is a wine connoisseur is an understatement. It is the only thing he knows. He not only loves wine, but produces it at the family-owned winery by the sea. Unfortunately for him, his scapegrace of a half-brother, Rick, doesn't share his refined sensibilities. Not only that, but he is getting married for the fourth time and needs money. He wants to sell the vineyard quickly, and divide the proceeds. Adrian refuses to let that happen, and he devises a fitting end to his brother's shallow life.

7. Tony Goodland, a compulsive gambler, is badly in need of money, but he can't touch his trust fund except in an emergency. His (apparently) solicitous Uncle Jarvis, who administers the fund, conceives of such an emergency – a fake kidnapping. Tony readily agrees to the plan, unaware that his trusted relative has his own secret agenda, with himself as the only beneficiary of the scheme.

The episode in the previous question aired on NBC. A very similar betrayal occurred in this ABC episode:

8. Beverly Hills jewelry store owner Leon Lamarr had been living on Easy Street for quite a while – until the latest recession, that is. His nephew, Freddy, a struggling photographer, has always relied on him to get through the tough times. One remarkable day, the tables turn suddenly when Leon gets a disastrous report from his stockbroker, and Freddy wins the lottery. But instead of being satisfied with the generous fee Freddy offers him to shield his bonanza from his estranged wife, the perfidious Uncle Leon wants the whole enchilada, and Freddy is betrayed and killed.

9. Which other episode involves a fake kidnapping, this time arranged by Leslie Williams, a lawyer who kills her husband? (She is also a pilot, and drops the ransom money from a plane.)

10. In this episode, the nephews are the traitors, not the uncle. Dexter and Norman Paris are twins. Dexter is a flamboyant celebrity chef on television; Norman is a much more reserved banker. The only quality they share is avarice. They have just been informed that their rich uncle plans to marry a much younger woman, and they see their inheritance fly out the window. Before the wedding can take place, one or both of them (I won't give it away) make sure that it never does.

11. It was definitely not one of her better days. Sex therapist and talk show host Dr. Joan Allenby was supposed to fly to Chicago that night, but the airport was fogged in, and she couldn't leave. Instead of going to a hotel, she returns to her office, hoping to find her boyfriend, David, there working late. He is there, all right, but he isn't working, unless rockin' and rollin' with her secretary is work. The scorned doctor carefully plans her revenge, and ends up killing the unfaithful David. (NOTE: The movie SLIDING DOORS has a similar setup, but no murder.)

12. This episode is another case of a nephew who values material possessions more than family togetherness. Art critic and television personality Dale Kingston wanted his wealthy uncle's world-class art collection so badly that he not only kills both his uncle and his girlfriend (who was an accessory, and could have exposed him), but tries to frame his sweet little old aunt for the crime.

13. Oliver Brandt's accounting partner discovers that he has been embezzling funds for years. He had to do it, he says, to keep his extravagant wife happy. But he gets no sympathy, and will soon be facing a prison term if he doesn't terminate the life of his overly inquisitive friend before he can blow the whistle on him.

14. Nora Chandler has a secret that only one person, her assistant, knows. She killed her cheating husband, a movie producer, years ago, and made it look like he simply vanished without a trace. When her assistant becomes engaged to a gossip columnist, Chandler fears that it is only a matter of time before she will spill the beans to her new husband, so Nora (reluctantly) kills her.

15. The motive in two episodes is nearly identical, even though the area of endeavor of the killers is different. In both cases, he is resting on his laurels, because someone else is the real creative force behind his work. The crisis comes when that person declares his intention to sever ties with him, which would reveal to everyone his own lack of talent. On NBC, the culprit is a writer; on ABC, he is a composer and orchestra conductor.

QUIZ 7.2: MOTIVES (Part 2) (‼)

1. In which of these episodes is the victim killed because he or she knows about a murder that was committed in the past (prior to the time frame of the show)? (Choose all that apply.)
   a. "Requiem for a Falling Star"
   b. "Murder, Smoke and Shadows"
   c. "Murder: A Self Portrait"
   d. "The Conspirators"
   e. "Old Fashioned Murder"

2. Most murders are committed for selfish, if understandable, reasons. The one in "Mind over Mayhem" is different. What motivates Dr. Marshall Cahill to kill Dr. Howard Nicholson, his colleague at the cybernetics institute?
   a. The desire to protect his protégé at the institute, Steven Spelberg
   b. The desire to protect his son, Neil
   c. Anger over Dr. Nicholson's unethical experiments
   d. Outrage at the institute's ties to corrupt foreign governments

3. Why does Dolores McCain kill her nephew, Harold, in "A Bird in the Hand..."? (He is the second victim in the show.)
   a. He threatens to tell Big Fred (her husband) about their affair.
   b. He is trying to thwart her control of the football team.
   c. He knows a secret from her life before she married his uncle.
   d. He suspects (and might be able to prove) that she was the driver who killed Big Fred in the hit-and-run that the police have called an accident.

4. In which of these episodes is greed the motive? (Choose all that apply.)
   a. "Double Shock"
   b. "Grand Deceptions"
   c. "Blueprint for Murder"
   d. "The Greenhouse Jungle"

5. In which of these episodes does a philandering husband kill his mistress because she is planning to reveal their affair to his wife? (Choose all that apply.)
   a. "Etude in Black"
   b. "Columbo and the Murder of a Rock Star"
   c. "Troubled Waters"
   d. "A Deadly State of Mind"
   e. "Murder in Malibu"

6. In which episode(s) does a husband kill his wife because she is domineering (in his opinion)?
   a. "A Friend in Deed"
   b. "Negative Reaction"
   c. "Swan Song"
   d. "Playback"
   e. "Fade in to Murder"

7. What drives architect Elliot Markham to kill Beau Williamson, a wealthy industrialist, in "Blueprint for Murder"?
   a. He is having an affair with Williamson's wife.
   b. Williamson cuts off funding for a project his wife had promised to bankroll while he was out of the country.
   c. Williamson threatens to report him to the Board of Architectural Review for using substandard materials.
   d. Williamson stole a design of his, and used it to build a complex which won critical acclaim.

8. Milo Janus is a health nut, and owns a chain of fitness clubs that bear his name. Why does he kill Gene Stafford, one of his franchisees, in "An Exercise in Fatality"?
   a. He caught Stafford stealing from the company.
   b. Stafford finds out that Janus sells drugs.
   c. Stafford has accused him of showing porn films to minors after hours.
   d. Stafford threatens to file a complaint about his unfair business practices.

9. In "It's All in the Game," conspirators Lauren Staton and Lisa Martin are responsible for whose murder?
   a. A man who is blackmailing them
   b. An employee who embezzled from their hair salon
   c. The lover they share, who is using one for her money and the other for her body
   d. The neighbor who had abused their daughters

10. Grace Wheeler is an aging (and senile) actress who kills
    her husband because he won't finance a return to the
    screen for her. Name the episode.
    a. "Forgotten Lady"
    b. "Requiem for a Falling Star"
    c. "Swan Song"
    d. "Lady in Waiting"

11. The motive for which of these women is, in part, indepen-
    dence from a domineering brother? (Choose all that
    apply.)
    a. Edna Brown ("Swan Song")
    b. Viveca Scott ("Lovely But Lethal")
    c. Kay Freestone ("Make Me a Perfect Murder")
    d. Ruth Lytton ("Old Fashioned Murder")
    e. Beth Chadwick ("Lady in Waiting")

12. He is a popular magician at a supper club. When the
    owner of the club recognizes him as former Nazi SS guard
    Stefan Mueller, he begins to blackmail him. Since the
    magician can't make him disappear, he believes that the
    only way to escape these invisible chains is to kill him.
    What is his stage name?
    a. Houdini's Second Act
    b. Garibaldi the Great
    c. The Great Santini
    d. Max the Magnificent

13. What is the title of the episode?
    a. "Now You See Him..."
    b. "Columbo Goes to the Guillotine"
    c. "Murder, Smoke and Shadows"
    d. "Mind Over Mayhem"

14. What is the name of the supper club?
    a. Sleight of Hand
    b. Illusions 'R' Us
    c. The Magic Castle
    d. The Cabaret of Magic

15. In which of these shows is the killer being blackmailed by the first victim? (Choose as many as apply.)
    a. "Double Exposure"
    b. "Fade in to Murder"
    c. "Columbo Likes the Nightlife"
    d. "Negative Reaction"
    e. "Troubled Waters"

16. Which of these philanderers kills his mistress because she threatens to expose their affair to his wife? (Choose all that apply.)
    a. Dr. Ray Fleming ("Prescription: Murder")
    b. Alex Benedict ("Etude in Black")
    c. Hayden Danziger ("Troubled Waters")
    d. Col. Frank Brailie ("Grand Deceptions")

17. Riley Greenleaf has two reasons for killing Alan Mallory, his star writer. What are they?
    a. He is defecting to another publisher.
    b. Mallory discovers that he cheats on his taxes.
    c. Mallory learns that he once killed a man in a bar fight.
    d. Greenleaf is the beneficiary in Mallory's life insurance policy.

QUIZ 7.3: Means (!!)

"Means" is "method," which usually refers to the weapon used. Because COLUMBO isn't a typical crime show, it also refers to a couple of unusual strategems. One title may be the answer to two or more questions. They are divided into NBC and ABC shows for convenience, but several questions have answers with at least one title from each network. All titles are used, except three, which are included as "red herrings."

NBC EPISODES

(a) "A Deadly State of Mind" (Nadia Donner)

(b) "Short Fuse"

(c) "How to Dial a Murder"

(d) "Murder Under Glass"

(e) "By Dawn's Early Light"

(f) "Double Shock" (Clifford Paris)

(g) "A Matter of Honor"

(h) "A Case of Immunity" (Youseff, the security guard)

(i) "Murder by the Book"

(j) "Suitable for Framing"

(k) "A Stitch in Crime" (Sharon Martin, the nurse)

(l) "Lovely But Lethal"

(m) "Identity Crisis" (Geronimo, the spy)

(n) "Dagger of the Mind" (Tanner, the butler)

(o) "Any Old Port in a Storm"

(p) "Publish or Perish" (Alan Mallory)

(q) "Requiem for a Falling Star"

(r) "Prescription: Murder"

(s) "Swan Song"

(t) "Try and Catch Me"

ABC EPISODES

(u) "Columbo Cries Wolf"

(v) "Grand Deceptions"

(w) "Columbo and the Death of a Rock Star"

(x) "Murder, Smoke and Shadows"

(y) "Columbo Goes to College"

(z) "Uneasy Lies the Crown"

(aa) "Columbo Likes the Nightlife"

(bb) "Ashes to Ashes" (Verity Chandler, the gossip writer)

1. In which NBC episode do the victims die in a plane crash?

2. In which episodes is a victim electrocuted? (One was on each network.)

3. In which one is the first victim (Karl Lessing) killed by a blow from a microscope? (It was on NBC.)

4. In which episode(s) is the weapon an animal?

5. In which NBC episode is the second victim, Tracy O'Connor, killed by a blow from a rock? (She was an accomplice in the first murder.)

6. In which episode(s) isn't the killer in the immediate vicinity of the victim when he or she dies? (Do not include cases where the killer takes a trip.)

7. In which episode(s) is the killer traveling when the victim dies? (Be careful.)

8. In which NBC show is the second victim killed by a blow from a champagne bottle (from which, ironically, she had just had a drink in celebration of her new romance)?

9. In which NBC episode does the victim (Vittorio Rossi) die by drinking from a poisoned wine bottle?

10. The case in the previous question is especially difficult for Columbo to solve, for two reasons. What are they?

11. In one NBC show, a medical procedure is used (potentially) to kill instead of heal. It doesn't succeed, because the doctor undoes his handiwork in time, after being warned by Columbo (who is uncharacteristically angry). What is the title?

12. What is the exceedingly clever trick by which Dr. Mayfield attempts to kill Dr. Hidemann, in that show? (He isn't killed by this or any other method, but there are two other victims, who are killed in different ways.)

13. In which episode(s) is the death of at least one victim caused by an incendiary device of some kind? (Be careful.)

14. Several episodes have fake suicides, but only one has a real suicide that is also a murder, because it is coerced. Which one? (It was on NBC.)

15. In which NBC episode is the victim killed by an exploding cannon? (This is ironic for the same reason as Q. 8.)

16. In which ABC show is the victim, Professor Rusk, shot by a gun triggered by remote control?

17. In which episode(s) is/are the victim(s) bludgeoned with a tire iron? (Not as high tech as the previous question.)

18. In which episode(s) is the victim found hanged, in an apparent suicide? (One was on NBC, the other was ABC.)

19. In which shows are the victims' necks broken by the killer? (Both were on ABC.)

20. In which one does the killer, Riley Greenleaf, hire a "hit man" to do away with his first victim? (The hit man soon becomes the second victim.)

ANSWERS
QUIZ 7.1

1. (c), (i), (k), (o)

2. (m); 3. (g); 4. (q); 5. (j)

6. (f) The method of Ric Carsini's death was undoubtedly inspired by Edgar Allan Poe's short story, "The Cask of Amontillado."

7. (a) Presumably, the title is a takeoff on THE BLACKBOARD JUNGLE (although there is no similarity between the plots).

8. (p); 9. (l); 10. (n); 11. (s); 12. (h); 13. (b)

14. (e) This episode is often misunderstood, and the blurb on the DVD is wrong. It says that Jerry Parks is Chandler's ex-husband, but they were never married, or even lovers. Whoever writes the synopses on the boxes really should watch the shows first. Many people believe that Parks was the intended victim of the car bombing, and that Jean was killed by mistake. That isn't true, but Chandler is counting on people making that assumption. No one would have any reason to kill Jean, so the police would dig deeper, and might uncover the truth. But Parks' death can easily be attributed to one of his many enemies.

15. (d), (c)

QUIZ 7.2

1. (a), (b) and (c)

2. (b) Dr. Nicholson has accused Neil Cahill of plagiarizing a paper written by a recently deceased scientist. His father kills Nicholson before he can make his charges public.

3. (d)

4. All except (b)

5. (a), (c)

6. (a), (b) and (c)

7. (b) He may be having an affair with Mrs. Williamson, also, but that is never made explicit.

8. (d)

9. (c) If "Hell hath no fury like a woman scorned," what about two women scorned?

10. (a)

11. (a), (d) and (e)

12. (c); 13. (a); 14. (d)

15. (b), (e). In (a) and (c) the killer is blackmailed by the second victim, who knows about the first murder.

16. (b), (c)

17. (a), (d)

QUIZ 7.3

1. (s)

2. (f), (x)

3. (l)

4. (c), (g)

5. (j)

6. (a), (b), (c), (e), (l)*, (o), (p), (s), (y), (z)
   (*the second victim, Shirley Blaine)

7. (t), (o). In (c), Mrs. Fleming is only injured in the assault. She dies later in the hospital after Dr. Fleming returns.

8. (i)

9. (d)

10. First, the poison that is used was from a Japanese puffer-fish (aka fugu), which the lab couldn't trace. Second, the poison was in the wine opener instead of the wine bottle. Columbo can't understand how a wine bottle picked at random out of dozens could have poison in it.

11. (k)

12. He uses dissolving suture in Dr. Hidemann's heart valve-replacement surgery, instead of the standard permanent suture. Dissolving suture is used only to close an incision, and keep it closed until the wound heals, after which it is not needed. It is a different color than permanent suture, to prevent accidental mistakes. Dr. Mayfield makes his deliberately.

13. (b) and (q). In (p), the victim is shot first, then blown up by his own homemade bomb. In (v), the victim is stabbed first, and then the body is placed in a hole with a land-mine.

14. (a) The victim does jump off her balcony, but only be-cause she had been hypnotized earlier and was responding to a post-hypnotic suggestion.

15. (e); 16. (y)

17. (a), (h), (k), (m)

18. (n), (aa). Both were actually strangled first, then hanged.

19. (u), (w); 20. (p)

PART EIGHT

THE PLOT THICKENS

QUIZ 8.1: RED HERRINGS

QUIZ 8.2: ACCIDENTS HAPPEN

QUIZ 8.3: FRAME-UPS

QUIZ 8.4: BOGUS ALIBIS

THE ART OF DECEPTION

The four quizzes in this section deal with the smokescreens Columbo has to see through to unmask a killer (or killers). The evildoers can be quite creative in their efforts to escape the consequences of their actions, and their schemes always involve some kind of deception. There are numerous variations, but most fall into six basic categories:

1. Trying to appear to be somewhere else, or claiming to have been somewhere else – known as an "alibi." The word, which is Latin, literally means "not at the place." An alibi means that the suspect couldn't have committed the crime because he or she wasn't there. We hear the word so often in connection with suspects who are found guilty that many people think it means a <u>phony</u> explanation, but that isn't true.

2. Pointing the finger at someone else – known as a frame-up. This strategy involves planting incriminating evidence on the premises, or in the vehicle, of the person who is to take the blame, or even on his or her person, although that is rare. A frame-up usually implicates a specific person, but it could also cast suspicion on a nebulous entity like the Mafia.

3. Making the homicide look like an accident or a suicide. This subterfuge may be the most likely to succeed, and it often takes a very astute coroner to see through it. Unless an autopsy is performed at the time, the truth may never be known, or isn't known for years, until an exhumation is ordered.

4. Committing the murder within the framework of a robbery, burglary, kidnapping, or act of vandalism.

5. Employing a proxy (i. e. – a "hit man") to do the deed. While this strategy can succeed, it is risky because there is someone else who knows about the crime, and that person can use his knowledge to blackmail whoever ordered the hit. This happens several times on COLUMBO (but with accomplices, not hit men).

6. Hiding or destroying the body, or rendering the victim impossible to identify, so that the police have a missing persons case on their hands, instead of a homicide.

QUIZ 8.1: Red Herrings (!!)

The best way to avoid being arrested for a murder is to make it look like something else. In this quiz, you decide which of the ruses listed below is utilized by the guilty party (or parties). If there are two murders but only one is relevant, the victim's name is given. The number of occurrences of each ruse (in the quiz, not the series) is noted beside it. The episodes are divided into two parts, one for NBC and one for ABC, but the list of deceptions is the same for both.

This theme is continued in QUIZ 8.2, which focuses on phony accidents and suicides. Frame-ups and fake alibis, two other popular deceptions, are covered in QUIZ 8.3 and QUIZ 8.4.

TYPES OF DECEPTION

(a) Apparent robbery (6)

(b) Apparent kidnapping (2)

(c) Apparent suicide (2)

(d) Apparent accident (7)*

(e) Apparent accidental shooting (1)

(f) Apparent mob hit or terrorist attack (2)

(g) Apparent heart attack (1)

(h) Apparent mugging (1)

(i) Apparent disappearance (1)

(j) Apparent accidental drowning (3)

(*Does not include any accidents listed separately.)

NBC EPISODES

1. "The Most Dangerous Match"
2. "Fade in to Murder"
3. "Ransom for a Dead Man"
4. "Dagger of the Mind" (Sir Roger Haversham)
5. "Candidate for Crime" (two possible answers)
6. "The Most Crucial Game"
7. "Old Fashioned Murder"
8. "By Dawn's Early Light"
9. "Identity Crisis"
10. "The Greenhouse Jungle" (Tony Goodland)
11. "Playback"
12. "Any Old Port in a Storm"
13. "The Bye-Bye Sky High IQ Murder Case"
14. "Try and Catch Me"
15. "Suitable for Framing" (Rudy Matthews)

ABC EPISODES

16. "Murder, Smoke and Shadows"
17. "Ashes to Ashes"
18. "Columbo Goes to College" (Professor Rusk)
19. "Uneasy Lies the Crown"
20. "Agenda for Murder"
21. "Murder: A Self Portrait"
22. "Rest in Peace, Mrs. Columbo"
23. "Death Hits the Jackpot"
24. "Caution: Murder Can Be Hazardous to Your Health"
25. "Columbo Likes the Nightlife" (Linwood Coben)

QUIZ 8.2: Accidents Happen (‼)

Many criminals on COLUMBO try to avert suspicion by staging the murder as an accident or a suicide. In this quiz, you have to match the episode to both the <u>apparent</u> cause of death and the <u>actual</u> cause of death. The name of the victim is provided for you, both as an aid to recall, and to identify the relevant murder, if there is more than one.

NOTE: Two or more murders can have the same actual cause of death, or the same apparent cause. All the choices in both lists are used.

1. "Murder by the Book" (Lily La Sanka)

2. "A Friend in Deed" (Margaret Halperin)

3. "Death Hits The Jackpot" (Freddy Brower)

4. "An Exercise in Fatality" (Gene Stafford)

5. "Any Old Port in a Storm" (Rick Carsini)

6. "The Most Crucial Game" (Eric Wagner)

7. "Uneasy Lies the Crown" (Adam Evans)*

8. "Lady in Waiting" (Bryce Chadwick)

9. "Publish or Perish" (Eddie Kane)

10. "Double Shock" (Clifford Paris)

11. "Etude in Black" (Jenifer Welles)

12. "Columbo Likes the Nightlife" (Linwood Coben)

13. "Agenda for Murder" (Frank Staplin)

14. "Grand Deceptions" (Sgt. Major Lester Keegan)

15. "Candidate for Crime" (Harry Stone)

16. "Caution: Murder Can Be Hazardous to Your Health" (Budd Clarke)

(*Two <u>apparent</u> causes for the same murder.)

APPARENT CAUSE OF DEATH

A. Suffered a heart attack while exercising

B. Drowned while scuba diving

C. Hit his head diving into the pool, and drowned

D. Slipped in the bathtub, and drowned

E. Had his windpipe crushed by a barbell in the gym

F. Thrown into the pool, and drowned

G. Shot by accident, in a case of mistaken identity

H. Heart attack caused by smoking too much

I. Died in a single car automobile accident

J. Suicide

K. Blown up by a landmine

L. Blown up by a homemade bomb

M. Drowned in a lake after boat capsized

ACTUAL CAUSE OF DEATH

(a) Forcibly drowned in the bathtub

(b) Intentionally shot

(c) Heart attack caused by digitalis poisoning

(d) Electrocuted

(e) Strangled

(f) Asphyxiated

(g) Bludgeoned with a heavy object

(h) Inhaled gas after being rendered unconscious

(i) Stabbed

(j) Heart attack caused by nicotine poisoning

QUIZ 8.3: FRAME-UPS (‼)

The more sinister of Columbo's suspects try to pin the murder on an innocent person, and the most sinister of all try to implicate someone near and (supposedly) dear to them. A frame-up can be a handy way of diverting suspicion, especially if you want to get rid of two people: kill one, and let the police take care of the other one. Columbo sees through these ruses fairly quickly most of the time, in spite of the perfidious perpetrators' premier efforts.

1. In "A Friend in Deed," Police Commissioner Mark Halperin wants his colleagues on the force to believe that his wife was really killed by whom?
   a. Hugh Caldwell, his next-door neighbor
   b. Artie Jessup, a cat burglar who has been active in the neighborhood
   c. An ex-con whom his wife has helped and befriended
   d. A serial killer who was recently in the news, and hasn't been caught

2. With her disagreeable brother out of the way, Ruth Lytton should be sitting pretty. Unfortunately, that persistent police Lieutenant isn't buying her story that he was killed accidentally in an attempted robbery. Now Ms. Lytton has to find someone to take the fall, so she plants an artifact (that she had reported stolen in the phony heist) in someone's clothes closet. Who is the unwitting victim of her nefarious scheme?
   a. Her niece, Janie
   b. Her older sister, Mrs. Brandt
   c. Her maid, Celeste
   d. Her next-door neighbor, Dorothy

3. What item supposedly stolen from the museum does she hide in that person's closet?
   a. A medieval brooch
   b. An antique belt buckle
   c. A 17th century cross
   d. A bag of ancient Roman coins

4. Dale Kingston plans the murder of his rich uncle as pains-takingly as humanly possible. He might be getting away with it, too, if a certain persistent detective didn't keep noticing a few meaningless incongruities. Instead of relishing his soon-to-be-acquired art collection, he has to divert the good Lieutenant's suspicions with another sus-pect. Where does he stash the two drawings by Degas that he took from his uncle's house after the murder?
   a. In his Aunt Edna's house
   b. In his girlfriend Tracy's apartment
   c. In lawyer Frank Simpson's office
   d. In painter Sam Franklin's studio

5. Patrick Kinsley and Cathleen Calvert are weary of seeing each other only occasionally on the sly, so they decide to make life easier by eliminating her husband. They know that the spouse is always the first suspect the police look at, so instead of killing him, they play it safe by framing him for a murder, instead. Whom do they kill?
   a. His next door neighbor, with whom he argued recently
   b. An investment broker who is suing him
   c. A poker playing buddy to whom he owes a lot of money
   d. His bookmaker

NOTE: The choices for the remaining questions follow the quiz.

6. Nurse Sharon Martin is disturbed by an irregularity (not in the heartbeat) she sees during a heart valve operation performed by Dr. Barry Mayfield. Her probing questions about the procedure are making the doctor extremely uncomfortable. Deciding that he can't take a chance on her learning the truth, he kills her, and stages a mugging to cover his tracks. Whom does he intend for the police to suspect in her murder?

7. Whom does Paul Galesko try to frame for his wife's murder in "Negative Reaction"?

8. Who is the innocent victim in Colonel Rumford's diabolical plot to incriminate someone for the murder he commits in "By Dawn's Early Light"?

9. In "Mind Over Mayhem," Dr. Cahill thinks the police will chalk the murder of Dr. Nicholson up to whom?

10. Whom does Hayden Danziger intend to take the blame for the murder of his mistress in "Troubled Waters"?

11. Whom does Graham McVeigh choose as the fall guy when he kills his brother in "Strange Bedfellows"?

12. When lawyer Hugh Creighton strangles his girlfriend, Marcy, in "Columbo and the Murder of a Rock Star," he sets it up so that the police suspect whom? (And everyone does – except Columbo, of course.)

13. When his star author decides to defect to another publisher, Riley Greenleaf kills him and casts suspicion on whom? The episode is "Publish or Perish."

14. In "Old Fashioned Murder," who is the first person Ruth Lytton sets up to take the rap for her brother Edward's murder?

15. In "Double Exposure," when Dr. Bart Keppel shoots the man who is threatening to expose him, whom does he expect the police to accuse? (This question refers to the first murder.)

16. Who is the intended fall guy in "Fade in to Murder"?

17. Who is supposed to be blamed for the death of Jerry Winters, in "Butterfly in Shades of Grey"?

18. In "Suitable for Framing," the crime is supposed to be blamed on unknown art thieves. When Columbo doesn't buy that explanation, the killer is forced to frame someone else. Who?

19. In two episodes (one on each network) the frame-ups are unique, because the killer creates a fictitious character for himself or herself to become. That way the police will be looking for someone who doesn't exist.

    A. Who is meant to take the fall in "Identity Crisis"?

    B. Who is meant to take the fall in "Sex and the Married Detective"?

CHOICES

(a) A shadowy figure named Steinmetz

(b) Alvin Deschler, ex-con

(c) Her drug-addicted ex-boyfriend

(d) Eddie Kane, homemade bomb enthusiast

(e) A call girl (or courtesan) named "Lisa"

(f) Ted Malloy, the victim's gay boyfriend

(g) Edna Matthews, the killer's aunt

(h) Neddy Malcolm, rock musician

(i) Lloyd Harrington, lounge pianist

(j) Mrs. Norris, the wife of a client

(k) The guard at the museum

(l) Sid Daley, the victim's husband

(m) Cadet Roy Springer

(n) Bruno Romano, a bookmaker

(o) An anonymous heroin user

QUIZ 8.4: Bogus Alibis (!!)

The third element of any homicide (besides motive and means) is opportunity, the absence of which is an alibi. The murderers on COLUMBO often go to great lengths to establish fake ones, and many are quite clever about it. But not quite as clever as Columbo is in exposing them.

Match each episode to one of the "foolproof" plans.

(a) "Make Me a Perfect Murder"

(b) "Suitable for Framing"

(c) "Playback"

(d) "Murder: A Self Portrait"

(e) "It's All in the Game"

(f) "Caution: Murder Can Be Hazardous to Your Health"

(g) "Columbo Cries Wolf"

(h) "Fade in to Murder"

1. Harold Van Wyck is a gadget-obsessed electronics wizard with the best security system money can buy. Hours before he kills his mother-in-law, he videotapes the empty room where it is going to happen. Minutes before he commits it, he turns off the security camera, and plays the tape of the empty room into the closed-circuit television in the guard house. Using a different VCR, he videotapes the murder, carefully staying outside the range of the camera in the room. After switching the system back to live recording, he puts the tape of the murder in the VCR, and programs it to play after he has left the house for a party. When the guard sees the tape of the murder, he will be miles away and well beyond the reach of the long arm of the law. (That is the plan, anyway.)

2. On Saturday, before going to Budd Clarke's house to kill him, Wade Anders stops by his production office. He retrieves the surveillance tape showing the previous evening (when he had been there) and that morning, when he arrived. Using a blank tape, he reverses the morning and evening footage, so that it appears to show that he was in his office all day Saturday. (Although ingenious, this alibi is clearly a rip-off of the one in the first question.)

3. A slight variation on those two alibis is used in another show. This time, the killer invites a friend over to watch a ball game on television. When he arrives, the killer slips him a Mickey. They watch the game for awhile, until the friend falls asleep. The killer then sets his VCR to record the game, and leaves the house. When he returns, the game is over, and he rewinds the tape. The last step is to press "play" and wake his friend up. Because the game is still on, apparently, the friend thinks that he couldn't have been asleep long, and he will testify that the killer didn't have enough time to commit the murder. (He gets caught, anyway, but it was still a nice try.)

4. Max Barsini devises what he thinks is the perfect alibi for murdering his ex-wife. When they were first married, they lived in a studio (literally) apartment over an Italian bar and restaurant in L. A. called Vito's. He revisits the place and renews his friendship with the owner. He tells Vito that he wants to paint a picture of his establishment, and make it a gift. Now that he is famous, he says, the painting should bring in many new customers. His only requirement is that he be allowed to paint it in his old loft, with no interruptions. Vito is delighted, of course, and agrees to the arrangement. Shortly thereafter, Barsini sneaks out the fire escape and drives to the beach, where he finds his ex-wife sunbathing. He knocks her out with chloroform, and dumps her in the ocean, unconscious. She drowns, and he returns to his studio. Everything goes exactly as planned: his ex-wife is dead, and Vito can testify that he couldn't have killed her because he was painting at the restaurant when it happened. (But there is a fly in the ointment, and its name is "Columbo.")

5. In which episode does the killer tinker with the counter on a projector to cover her tracks?

6. In which two episodes does the killer (or killers) use an electric blanket to delay the cooling of the body?

7. There is a unique twist on the bogus alibi concept in one ABC episode. Instead of disguising a murder as a disappearance, this killer and his accomplice try to make a disappearance look like a murder. They hope that the publicity will help the sales of their magazine, which will in turn drive up the price when they sell it. They get all the publicity they can handle, but then things turn sour, and the accomplice is killed (for real, this time).

✳✳✳✳✳✳✳

8. In "Suitable for Framing," what do Dale Kingston and a female accomplice do to make it appear as if he couldn't have killed his rich uncle? (Choose all that apply.)
   a. He calls his uncle from a friend's house and pretends to speak to him, loudly enough so the friend will hear.
   b. His partner, in high-heeled shoes, runs down the stone steps behind the house to fool the rent-a-cop in front of the house.
   c. He claims to have lost a cufflink, and asks the car parking attendant to help him look for it in his trunk.
   d. He goes to a public place, and repeatedly asks the time.

9. Where is he when the burglar alarm alerts the security guard?
   a. Chez Louis, a French restaurant
   b. A bar called The Blue Martini
   c. An art gallery
   d. The television studio where he tapes his program
   e. A movie premiere

10. When Columbo interrogates Van Wyck after the murder,* he watches the tape of it and comments on how unfortunate it is that the killer stayed just outside of the camera's vision. When Van Wyck agrees, Columbo opines that it is almost impossible to believe. What does Van Wyck say about the placement of the camera, in order to allay his suspicions? (*See Question 1)

ANSWERS
QUIZ 8.1

1. (d); 2. (a); 3. (b); 4. (d)
5. (e) or (f)
6. (j); 7. (a); 8. (d)
9. (c); 10. (b); 11. (a)
12. (j); 13. (a); 14. (d)
15. (a); 16. (d); 17. (i)
18. (f); 19. (d); 20. (c)
21. (d); 22. (a); 23. (j)
24. (g); 25. (c)

QUIZ 8.2

1. M, (g) / 2. F, (a)
3. D, (a) / 4. E, (e)
5. B, (f) / 6. C, (g)
7. I, (c) / 8. G, (b)
9. L, (b) / 10. A, (d)
11. J, (h) / 12. J, (e)
13. J, (b) / 14. K, (i)
15. G, (b) / 16. H, (j)

QUIZ 8.3

1. (b)

2. (a) Columbo's act of escorting her from the house on his arm when she is arrested clearly portrays Ruth Lytton as a sympathetic figure. But don't forget that she actually tries to frame her own niece, who was devoted to her.

3. (b)

4. (a) Dale Kingston is a totally unsympathetic character, but it is still hard to understand how he could frame his own aunt. He and Ruth Lytton would be great together.

5. (b); 6. (c)

7. (b); 8. (m)

9. (o); 10. (i)

11. (n); 12. (h)

13. (d); 14. (k)

15. (j); 16. (l)

17. (f); 18. (g)

19A. (a); 19B. (e)

QUIZ 8.4

1. (c); 2. (f); 3. (h); 4. (d)

5. (a); 6. (b), (e); 7. (g)

8. All except (a).

9. (c)

10. He says that the camera was only supposed to record the safe, not the whole room, because they were anticipating a possible burglar, not a murderer.

PART NINE

THE INVESTIGATIONS

QUIZ 9.1: RED FLAGS

QUIZ 9.2: ALIBI BUSTERS

QUIZ 9.3: A FEW TRICKS

THE ART OF DETECTION

By his own admission, one reason for Columbo's success in apprehending criminals is his attention to small details, especially those that don't seem to fit. In many cases, this awareness prevents him from accepting the seemingly obvious solution to the crime, much to the annoyance of his superiors. He shares this propensity with another highly effective (and even more eccentric) sleuth – Agatha Christie's Hercule Poirot. (Poirot has no superiors, so there is no one to object to his behavior. However, he does occasionally assist the police, and in many of those situations the same dynamic is present. The conscientious but dull-witted policemen see the case as "open and shut," and want to wrap it up quickly. They are baffled and frustrated by Poirot's doubts – but Poirot, naturally, always turns out to have been right.)

This section focuses on the clues and red flags that lead to the unmasking of some brilliant, but doomed, murderers.

QUIZ 9.1: Red Flags (!)

These questions are related to episodes in which the homicide is made to look like an accident or suicide, or a kidnapping or robbery that goes wrong. In each case, there is at least one "red flag" that leads Columbo to suspect that the death might not be what it appears to be, or have been caused by what (or who) apparently caused it. A red flag is generally not the coup de grace that seals the culprit's fate; it just creates doubt in Columbo's mind.

Select the relevant keyword or key phrase. Details are given with the answers.

(a) His taste in music

(b) Shoelaces

(c) Lights

(d) No nickel

(e) A broken pipe

(f) Reading glasses

(g) A burned match

(h) "Hello"

(i) No chlorine

(j) A fountain change

(k) Worthless paintings

(l) Women's panties

(m) An overturned book

(n) Fake diamonds

(o) Clipped cigars

(p) A joke

(q) Shoe polish

1. In "Old Fashioned Murder," Edward Lytton and a security guard are both found dead in the museum. Edward had been doing an inventory late at night. It appeared that the guard, who was off-duty, had returned to the museum after hours to burgle it, and that he and Edward shot and killed each other. What does Columbo notice as soon as he enters the room, that causes him to doubt that scenario?

2. In "Prescription: Murder," Dr. Fleming kills his wife in their apartment, then leaves on a cruise with his mistress. Columbo is called to the scene after the attack is reported (at this point it is only attempted murder), and he is there when Fleming returns from his trip. What doesn't Fleming do that seems odd to Columbo at the time?

3. In "An Exercise in Fatality," Milo Janus wants it to appear that his victim died while working out at the gym, after it was closed, because he tried to lift a barbell that was too heavy for him, and it crushed his windpipe. What tiny but significant detail tells Columbo that the man was murdered?

4. That clue was used again, with a minor variation, in an ABC episode. The victim, Theresa Goren, clearly did not dress herself, and whoever dressed her must be a man. (He is, in fact, Wayne Jennings.) How does Columbo know this?

5. What contributes to Elliott Markham's undoing in "Blueprint for Murder"?

6. What clue is responsible for Nora Chandler's downfall in "Requiem for a Falling Star"?

7. What makes Columbo suspicious of Dale Kingston's claim, in "Suitable for Framing," that his uncle was killed during a robbery?

8. Sir Roger Haversham was killed (during an argument) in a dressing room at the theater, but the responsible parties transport his body in a trunk back to his estate, where they arrange it so that he appears to have fallen down a long flight of stairs. What two details cause Columbo to see red in "Dagger of the Mind"?

9. In "Agenda for Murder," the murder is staged as a suicide. What clue involving a fax machine makes Columbo question that scenario?

10. In "A Friend in Deed," how does Columbo know that cat burglar Artie Jessup (the prime suspect) couldn't possibly be the killer they are looking for?

11. In the same episode, what evidence confirms that Mrs. Halperin did not drown in the swimming pool, as it appears she did?

12. In "Mind Over Mayhem," what two clues convince Columbo that Dr. Nicholson didn't die inside his house, where the body is found? (One is found in the driveway; the other, inside the house.)

13. What does Columbo find in the house that indicates who the killer might be? (He doesn't have a suspect yet, but he knows what type of person to look for because of this clue.)

14. What nearly identical clue is used in "A Trace of Murder"?

15. In "Double Exposure," Columbo suspects that Dr. Keppel killed a projectionist who tried to blackmail him. What clue that confirms his suspicions, does he find at the theater where the victim worked?

QUIZ 9.2: Alibi Busters (‼)

No choices are provided for these questions, but hints are given for most of them.

1. Dale Kingston's alibi in "Suitable for Framing" seems air-tight. Why is Columbo suspicious of it?

2. Harold Van Wick's alibi scheme in "Playback" is probably the most ingenious ruse in all the episodes. Why does it fail? (Hint: RSVP)

3. Wade Anders' alibi in "Caution: Murder Can Be Hazardous to Your Health" is designed the same way as Van Wick's, but in spite of his cleverness, the tape is exposed as a hoax. How? (Think about gardening.)

4. In "By Dawn's Early Light," Colonel Lyle Rumford tries to pin the explosion on a cadet who was responsible for cleaning the cannon in preparation for its use in the Founder's Day ceremony. Why doesn't the accusation stick? (Dereliction of duty.)

5. Viveca Scott has a bad case of poison ivy in "Lovely But Lethal." How does that place her at the scene of the first murder? (It relates to the weapon she uses.)

6. What does Oscar Finch do, in "Agenda for Murder," that definitely places him at the scene of the crime? (He was hungry.)

7. In "Murder: A Self Portrait," what two clues enable Columbo to puncture Max Barsini's alibi? (One relates to brushes; the other, to paint splotches.)

8. How does Columbo see through Nelson Brenner's clever alibi in "Identity Crisis"? (It relates to a news event.)

9. In "Swan Song," what does Columbo learn about Tommy Brown's military training that points him in the right direction?

10. Why does Columbo suspect that Adrian Carsini isn't being truthful in "Any Old Port in a Storm"? (Ric's car is a convertible.)

11. What seemingly minor detail in "Dagger of the Mind" puts Columbo hot on the trail of Nicholas Frame and Lillian Stanhope? ("Raindrops keep fallin' on my head...")

12. In "Columbo Cries Wolf," after Dian Hunter disappears the second time, Sean Brantley shows Columbo a surveillance tape of a woman leaving the compound in a car. He says it is Dian, but Columbo notices something that convinces him otherwise. (Think high-tech jewelry.)

13. True or False? The clue in Question 6 was found in a police magazine.

QUIZ 9.3: A Few Tricks (‼)

"IT TAKES A DECEIVER TO CATCH A DECEIVER"

Most of the time, dogged persistence and a keen eye for the incongruous are sufficient for Columbo to crack the case. However, some of the cleverer and more elusive killers force the shrewd detective to be creative and employ subterfuge of his own. Here are some examples of Columbo's talent for deception.

1. How does Columbo trick Paul Galesko (Dick Van Dyke) into exposing himself as the murderer in "Negative Reaction"?

2. What ruse does Columbo employ in "Death Lends a Hand" to trick Brimmer (Robert Culp)?

3. What elaborate scheme does Columbo conceive to expose Mark Halperin (Richard Kiley) as the killer in "A Friend in Deed"?

4. How does Columbo prove that art critic Dale Kingston (Ross Martin) is the killer in "Suitable for Framing"?

5. How does Columbo trap Dr. Keppel in "Double Exposure"?

6. Columbo uses a Shriner's ring to dupe one killer into returning to her house to see if her husband's body has been disturbed. When she does as he expects, he is there waiting for her. Name the killer and the episode.

7. This trick doesn't prove anyone guilty, but it does advance the investigation. How does Columbo determine that Janie couldn't have been the killer in "Old Fashioned Murder"? (It is an experiment involving something that was supposedly stolen from the museum.)

8. In "Short Fuse," Columbo goes on a ride in a cable car with the killer, Roger Stanford. When they are halfway up the mountain, Columbo shows him something he brought with him. Before long, Stanford panics and begs Columbo to throw it out the window. What is it?

9. Columbo is one dedicated civil servant. In three episodes, he risks certain death to prove his case, by enticing the primary suspect to make an attempt on his life. It works, but if his guess had been wrong, or his preparations had failed, he would have become a victim himself – and somebody else would have been assigned to investigate <u>his</u> murder.

   A. How does Columbo get Dr. Mason ("How to Dial a Murder") to reveal himself?

   B. He uses a similar gambit in "Murder Under Glass." What does he do in that episode?

   C. It worked twice before, so he does basically the same thing in "Columbo Goes to the Guillotine." What is the scheme this time?

10. True or False? The elusive Mrs. Columbo dies by eating from a poisoned jar of lemon marmalade in "Rest in Peace, Mrs. Columbo."

ANSWERS
QUIZ 9.1

1. (c) The lights are off. Since Edward was working at night, the lights must have been on. If he and the guard are the only ones in the room, and both of them are dead, who turned the lights off? Ruth Lytton, the real killer, is who. She is compulsively frugal, and turned them off by habit.

2. (h) When he unlocks the door to his apartment, he doesn't call out to his wife, as anyone would be expected to do. The reason he doesn't, of course, is that he thinks she is dead. [There is an identical scene in the movie THE THIN MAN GOES HOME, and it is a red flag for Nick Charles. You can bet the farm that that is where Levinson and Link got the idea. Why let a great clue go to waste?]

3. (b) If he had tied his own shoes, the loops of the shoelaces would have been reversed. But he didn't tie his own shoes, or get himself dressed, because he was dead. After killing him, Janus removed his street clothes and attired him in a gym outfit.

4. (l) The killer had put her panties on backwards, and Columbo notices that the tag is on the wrong side.

5. (a) Markham is a classical music enthusiast. After he kills Beau Williamson, he puts the body in the trunk of Beau's car, and drives it to the shed where he is going to store it temporarily. While driving, he changes the radio station from country music (which Beau listens to, but which he hates) to classical. Columbo had been told that Beau hated every kind of music except country, so he deduces that Markham had something to do with Beau's disappearance.

6. (j) The fountain in her backyard doesn't have running water, because the husband she killed ten years earlier is buried under it. To run the fountain, the ground would have to be dug up, and the body would be found. That isn't the murder she is being investigated for, but Columbo connects it to the one she commits on the show, which is motivated by the need to protect the secret of the first one.

7. (k) Following the apparent burglary, Columbo notes that
   many valuable paintings were left behind, while some relatively worthless ones were taken. No self-respecting art
   thief would do that.

8. (f), (m) 1. If Sir Roger had really fallen down all those
   stairs, the reading glasses in his breast pocket would almost
   certainly have been broken, but they weren't. 2. Frame
   had placed Sir Roger's first edition of ALICE IN WONDER-
   LAND next to his easy chair to make it look as if he had
   been reading. But the book was open and turned over,
   which is bad for the spine. Nobody would do that to a
   valuable book he owns.

9. (p) The victim, Frank Staplin, had just faxed a joke to his
   wife, who was in Hawaii – dubious behavior for a suicidal
   person.

10. (n) The "diamonds" that Police Commissioner Halperin
    claims Artie Jessup took from the victim's house are found
    to be cubic zirconia. Since an experienced cat burglar like
    Artie would never have taken them, the evidence clears
    him of both the murder and the robbery. In other words,
    the frame-up backfires.

11. (i) If Margaret Halperin had drowned in the pool, she
    would have had chlorine in her lungs, but there wasn't
    any. There was only soap, which proves that she was
    really killed in the bathtub.

12. (e), (q) 1. A broken pipe is found in the driveway, where
    Dr. Nicholson was struck by the car driven by Dr. Cahill.
    2. Shoe polish is seen on the wall at chest height, indicat-
    ing that the body had been carried into the house.

13. (g) The match that Columbo finds in the living room
    ashtray had burned all the way, which points to a cigar
    smoker, because cigars take longer to light. (This is a
    "goof," because Dr. Nicholson smoked a pipe, which also
    takes longer to light.)

14. (o) Clifford Calvert, the prime suspect, is a cigar smoker.
    Columbo observes that the ends of the cigars he smokes
    are cut off differently from the ones that were collected at
    the crime scene, which had been left there to frame him.

15. (d) The victim had explained to Columbo that when he
    runs the projector, he always places a nickel at the end of
    the first roll of film. If he falls asleep, he will wake up
    when the nickel hits the concrete floor, and he can change
    the reels in time. When Columbo inspects the floor of the
    projection room, he doesn't find a nickel, so he knows that
    Dr. Keppel must have switched the reels after killing him.

QUIZ 9.2

1. Precisely because it is so good. Columbo says that most
   people seldom know exactly where they were at any given
   time.

2. Columbo repeatedly plays back the two tapes: the recording of the empty room, and the recording of the murder.
   After seeing nothing amiss, he has the frames progressive-
   ly enlarged until, finally, he spots a discrepancy. On the
   tape of the murder, he recognizes the invitation to the
   party that is Van Wick's alibi. That particular invitation
   had to be presented in person to gain admittance, meaning
   that Van Wick was still in the house at the time of the murder. As Robert Burns wisely said, "The best-laid schemes
   of mice and men go aft astray." (And rats, in this case.)

3. The hedges outside the front door are neatly trimmed in
   the morning footage, and overgrown in the evening
   footage, because they were cut Saturday morning after he
   leaves the office. The gardener told him he was going to
   trim the bushes, but he either forgot about that, or didn't
   think they would be visible on the tape.

4. Rumford claims that the cadet must have accidentally left
   his cleaning rag in the cannon, but he was off-campus
   seeing his girlfriend, and never cleaned it.

5. She got the poison ivy from a slide on the microscope that
   she bludgeons Karl Lessing with. Poison ivy (according to
   Columbo's nephew) doesn't grow in Los Angeles, and
   Columbo surmises that the rash might be connected to the
   murder. His hunch is confirmed when he gets a case of it
   himself after touching the glass fragments on Lessing's
   carpet.

6. He takes a bite from a hunk of cheese on the victim's desk, and a forensic dentist determines that the bite marks match Finch's dental records. Bite mark evidence really is used to solve crimes; serial killer Ted Bundy was convicted with it.

7. In two ways, actually. Columbo finds that the sink in the studio hasn't been used in months, so Barsini couldn't have cleaned his brushes there. And there are no paint spatters below the easel, unlike the easels at his house (which is where he actually painted the picture several days earlier).

8. Brenner claims that he couldn't have killed Geronimo because he was in his office all evening preparing a speech he was to give the next day. He even gives Columbo a copy of the speech to prove it. But in the speech he mentions that the Chinese pulled out of the Olympics, which didn't happen until the following day, so he couldn't have dictated it when he says he did.

9. Columbo learns that he was an expert parachute rigger in the Army. He packs a chute into the pouch that is supposed to carry flight charts, and parachutes to safety. But his two victims, who had been drugged, die when the plane crashes.

10. Adrian claims that his brother Ric drowned while scuba diving. But it had rained that day, and the top was down on Ric's convertible. If Ric had driven the car on the day Adrian says he did, the top would have been up. (It was really Adrian who drove the car, but the day he drove it, it wasn't raining, so he didn't put the top up.)

11. The roof of Sir Roger's car had water spots on it. It had rained in London, but not at his estate, which indicates that he could have gone to London, and might have been killed there. He was known to be a patron of Frame's and Stanhope's, and they were appearing in London, so the investigation started with them. That wasn't a lot to go on, but this is fiction, after all.

12. Sean Brantley's current flame, Tina, leaves the compound dressed exactly as Dian Hunter, except for one thing: she isn't wearing the beeper bracelet that matches the one Sean wears. He had told Columbo that neither of them is ever without it.

13. True. Peter Falk came across it while waiting in a doctor's office.

QUIZ 9.3

1. Columbo intentionally reverses the negatives found on the camera Galesko used to take pictures of his wife after he kidnapped her. A clock in the photographs shows a time when Galesko doesn't have an alibi. The only way for him to exonerate himself is to prove that Columbo made a mistake. To do that, he needs the camera, which he shouldn't be able to recognize, since he claims that someone else took the pictures. When he selects the right one from a group of cameras, the game is over.

2. He tells Brimmer that the victim's body is missing a contact lens. He expects him to look for it in his car trunk and reveal himself, which is exactly what he does. (She really hadn't lost one.)

3. Halperin, who is the Deputy Police Commissioner, has been trying to implicate a well-known cat burglar in the murder that he, himself, committed. Columbo gives Halperin his own address as the burglar's, and tricks him into planting evidence there.

4. After the murder, Kingston takes two Degas drawings from his uncle's house, and entrusts them to his accomplice. He retrieves them from her later, but when he returns to his apartment, he runs into Columbo, who was waiting for him. Columbo wants to know what is in the portfolio he is carrying, and Kingston says that it contains some drawings he was asked to evaluate. Columbo asks if he can look at them, and reaches inside. Kingston stops him, but not before he touches the drawings. When they turn up later and are dusted for fingerprints, Columbo's are found on them, which proves that they are the drawings Kingston had in his portfolio, and he must have taken them.

5. He turns the tables on him, so to speak, by using "subliminal cuts." He has photographs taken of himself looking for the gun, and splices them into film footage Keppel is going to see. It makes Keppel uncomfortable, and he goes to where the calibration converter is hidden, revealing it, and himself.

6. Nora Chandler, in "Requiem for a Falling Star." Columbo suspects that she killed her cheating husband 10 years earlier, and buried him in the yard. When he learns that her husband was a member of the Masonic Temple, he borrows a Shriner's ring and pays a messenger to deliver it to her in an envelope. She figures that someone must have exhumed the body and taken the ring (for blackmailing purposes, presumably.)

7. Ruth Lytton, the killer, shows Columbo an antique belt buckle that is found in her niece Janie's closet, which (she says) went missing from the museum after the murder. He is pretty sure Janie is being framed. To prove it, he takes the belt buckle, and a gift of fast food, with him when he goes to the jail to interview her. He sets the hamburgers and the artifact next to her on the bed, and she takes out a cigarette. When she is through smoking, she puts it out on the belt buckle. Obviously she doesn't recognize it as valuable museum property, and Columbo knows he is right.

8. The victim was killed by an exploding cigar, so Columbo brings an identical box of cigars (the non-exploding kind) with him on the trip. Since the killer has no way of knowing that it is a different box, he freaks out – and, unable to account for his erratic behavior, he confesses.

9A. Dr. Mason trained his two Dobermans to attack and kill when he says the word "Rosebud" – something Columbo learns fortuitously when the dogs are quarantined at the police station. A trainer at an animal obedience school informs him that the dogs can be reprogrammed so that they respond to the same command in a totally different way. With the trainer's help, Columbo trains the dogs to be affectionate instead of aggressive, when they hear the command word. When he confronts Dr. Mason with the evidence he has against him, the suspect says "Rosebud" and points at Columbo. To Columbo's relief, the dogs lick him, instead of mauling him.

9B. The victim died from an unknown poison, which Columbo initially thinks was in a wine bottle he drank from. But he learns that the victim chose a bottle at random from a large cellar, so that would have been impossible. Eventually he concludes that the poison was in the wine bottle opener, instead – the kind that uses a cartridge. At the invitation of Paul Gerard (the suspect), Columbo cooks a meal for the two of them, and they share two bottles of wine. Columbo has a hunch that Gerard is going to try to kill him the same way he killed the victim, so he brings his own opener, which he identifies with a small mark. Columbo opens the first bottle with his opener. Gerard opens the second one, after which Columbo looks at the opener and sees that it isn't marked. After the wine is poured, he switches their glasses when Gerard's back is turned. Just before Gerard drinks his wine, Columbo takes it from him and explains that he switched the glasses, and he will be taking his tainted one to the crime lab.

9C. A guillotine blade can be oriented two ways: in one position, it chops your head off; turned around, nothing happens. The positions are marked "Safe" and "Not Safe" for the benefit of the magician, who (we assume) doesn't have a death wish. After learning all of this from an amateur magician, Columbo asks the killer to meet him at the crime scene, saying that he needs his help. Before he arrives, Columbo reverses the labels on the guillotine. When he arrives, Columbo asks him to demonstrate it for him, and he sticks his head inside the apparatus. The suspect places the blade in the "Not Safe" position (which is actually the "Safe" position, because the labels are reversed), and pulls the release lever. If Columbo had miscalculated, and the suspect really hadn't intended to kill him, then (ironically) he would have been killed, and the series would have been cancelled prematurely – after only one episode. (It was the first one shown on ABC.)

10. False. Columbo suspects that Ms. Dimitri is up to no good when she gives him a jar of marmalade to take to his wife, so he takes it instead to the crime lab, where it is found to be poisoned. Then he hosts a phony funeral for the deceased Mrs. Columbo, which Ms. Dimitri attends. Afterward, he invites her to his house and pretends to be sick himself. When he appears to be at death's door, she feels that it is safe to confess (and even gloat).

PART TEN

POTPOURRI

QUIZ 10.1: TRIVIA

QUIZ 10.2: QUOTATIONS

QUIZ 10.3: RECYCLING CAN BE FUN

QUIZ 10.4: CROSSWORD PUZZLE

QUIZ 10.5: IN OTHER WORDS

QUIZ 10.1: Trivia (!)

Why, you ask, is there a quiz on trivia?. Isn't the entire book about trivia? By way of explanation, I offer these observations:

Like "noise," what "trivia" is depends on one's point of view. In other words, it is subjective. To paraphrase the cliché about beauty, "trivia is in the mind of the beholder." After all, which facts are truly vital? Your birthday, for one – try applying for a job or Social Security without knowing it. If you are a married man, your wife's birthday is equally important, unless you enjoy sleeping on the couch. Your IQ matters, if you want to join Mensa. After that, the significance of most facts is relative – to the beholder, and to other facts.

Most Americans would agree that it is important to know the names of the Presidents, at least the ones on Mt. Rushmore. But a Briton would undoubtedly place the knowledge of English kings higher on the scale of importance, and a Filipino wouldn't care about either list. Even if we limit the discussion to one country, the triviality of many facts is open to debate. For an American, the fact that Lincoln was a President is surely worth knowing. The fact that he was President during the Civil War is also significant. What about the fact that he was the 16th President? An American History teacher would certainly think so, and most other Americans would probably agree. How about the fact that he was the tallest President (tied with Bill Clinton)? At this point, many people are likely to say, "no, that is trivial." Transitioning from history to science, is the fact that bacteria cause disease trivial, or important? If you want to stay healthy, it is unquestionably important. Is it important to know that this fact was discovered by Louis Pasteur? That knowledge won't help you stay healthy, and it isn't likely to help you in any other way, either (unless you are on Jeopardy), so a majority of people would probably consider it trivial. They could be right, but anyone interested in the history of medicine would see the question very differently.

With regard to COLUMBO, there is clearly a hierarchy of significance concerning the details. The identity of the killer is the most important, of course, even though we know that from the start in a majority of the episodes. The identity of the victim and the motive, are probably next in importance. In the real world, how the crime was committed doesn't matter so much, but it assumes greater meaning on COLUMBO because so many of the murders involve deceptions. The weapon is relatively trivial, but in cases where it is unusual, or helps to identify the killer, it can be more significant.

Yes, every question in this book is a "trivia" question, but the ones in this quiz are probably more trivial than the rest. On the other hand, one man's trivia is another man's fact. In the eyes of trivia lovers, trivia is never really trivial.

1. Columbo often talks about his nephew (whose existence some people have doubted). He tells one murder suspect that his nephew has very thick glasses, and that the man is his nephew's idol. Who is he?

2. What are the names of Dr. Mason's Dobermans in "How to Dial a Murder"?
   a. Mutt and Jeff
   b. Hansel and Gretel
   c. Laurel and Hardy
   d. Flotsam and Jetsam

3. In "An Exercise in Fatality," what makes interrogating Milo Janus (Robert Conrad) especially arduous?
   a. Columbo has to keep up with him on his morning run (wearing his raincoat, no less).
   b. He asks Columbo to help him move a pile of bricks.
   c. Columbo has to lift weights with him.
   d. He challenges Columbo to arm wrestle.

4. In "The Most Dangerous Match," what disease does Tomlin Dudek have that causes his manager to keep him on a short leash?
   a. Asthma
   b. Fainting spells
   c. Cardiac arrhythmias
   d. Diabetes

5. Who was the previous owner of the seriously bent pool cue
   that Columbo tries out at Dr. Mason's house?
   a. John Barrymore
   b. Nelson Eddy
   c. W. C. Fields
   d. Orson Welles

6. What is the name of the high-IQ club in THE BYE-BYE SKY
   HIGH IQ MURDER CASE?
   a. Mensa
   b. The Sigma Society
   c. Phi Beta Kappa
   d. Geniuses, Inc.

7. What is the name of the fictional mystery writer in the
   books written by Ken Franklin and Jim Ferris in "Murder by
   the Book"?
   a. Mrs. Marlow
   b. Miss Poirot
   c. Ms. Simon
   d. Mrs. Melville

8. What symphony does Alex Benedict conduct in "Etude in
   Black"?
   a. Beethoven's Ninth Symphony
   b. Mozart's Jupiter Symphony
   c. Berlioz's Symphonie Fantastique
   d. Brahms' Third Symphony

9. What famous singer and musician has a cameo role in
   "Columbo and the Murder of a Rock Star"?
   a. Jerry Lee Lewis
   b. Little Richard
   c. Roy Orbison
   d. Bo Diddley

10. In which episode does Columbo get into a fender-bender
    with the suspect?
    a. "Caution: Murder Can Be Hazardous to Your Health"
    b. "Agenda for Murder"
    c. "A Deadly State of Mind"
    d. "Murder in Malibu"

11. In "Forgotten Lady," what is the title of the musical that Grace Wheeler (Janet Leigh) is watching at the end of the show? (It is one that Wheeler had starred in.)
    a. BYE BYE BIRDIE
    b. MY FAIR LADY
    c. CAROUSEL
    d. WALKING MY BABY

12. What is the name of the football team Eric Wagner (Dean Stockwell) owns in "The Most Crucial Game"?
    a. The Los Angeles Rockets
    b. The Burbank Bobcats
    c. The Whittier Wolves
    d. The Sacramento Stallions

13. In "The Conspirators," what is the slogan that Joe Devlin (Clive Revill) says to himself whenever he drinks from a bottle of whiskey?
    a. "Erin Go Bragh"
    b. "Shiver me timbers"
    c. "This far, no farther"
    d. "In a pig's eye"

14. What object does Columbo insert into the tailpipe of Brimmer's car to disable it, in "Death Lends a Hand"?
    a. Wadded up newspaper
    b. A dishrag
    c. A ball of string
    d. A potato

15. After Dale Kingston (Ross Martin) kills his uncle, he takes a number of valuable paintings off the wall, and tosses them on the floor. But he carefully wraps, and places in a portfolio, two pastel sketches by a famous French artist. These he gives to his accomplice for safe keeping. Who is the artist, and what are the drawings worth? The episode is "Suitable for Framing."
    a. Monet ($1,000,000)
    b. Toulouse-Lautrec ($50,000)
    c. Degas ($150,000)
    d. Pissarro ($75,000)

16. What humble food plays a pivotal role in "Agenda for Murder"?
    a. A carrot
    b. A piece of cheese
    c. A cracker
    d. An onion

17. In that same episode, what does the secretary give Columbo as a present for his wife?
    a. A can of air freshener
    b. A bouquet of flowers
    c. A recipe for chocolate cake
    d. An aerial photograph of Paris

18. When Columbo meets Lisa Chambers (Clifford Paris' fiancee) in "Double Shock," what is she doing that makes him uncomfortable?
    a. Swimming
    b. Getting dressed for a party
    c. Waxing her legs
    d. Yoga

19. Where do Dudek and Clayton play an impromptu private chess game on the eve of their internationally publicized match, in "The Most Dangerous Match"?
    a. In the hotel lobby
    b. In the park across the street from the hotel
    c. In an out-of-the-way French restaurant
    d. In Dudek's hotel room

20. In "Try and Catch Me," what does Abigail Mitchell (Ruth Gordon) ask Columbo to do, that he only agrees to after a lot of coaxing?
    a. Take her dog for a walk
    b. Say a few words to her women's group about his job
    c. Peel the onions she is cooking for dinner
    d. Fix her stopped up sink

QUIZ 10.2: QUOTATIONS (‼)

1. Who threatens Columbo with the line, "I'll have your badge, my friend."?
   a. Mark Halperin, in "A Friend in Deed"
   b. Maj. Gen. Martin Hollister, in "Dead Weight"
   c. Col. Frank Brailie, in "Grand Deceptions"
   d. Dr. Bart Keppel, in "Double Exposure"

2. When Jerry Parks, a gossip columnist she despises, points to his temple, which actress says, "You couldn't get bus fare for what is up there."
   a. Grace Wheeler in "Forgotten Lady"
   b. Lillian Stanhope, in "Dagger of the Mind"
   c. Nora Chandler, in "Requiem for a Falling Star"

3. Who says about his secretary: "She's quite the Iron Maiden"?
   a. Milo Janus, in "An Exercise in Fatality"
   b. Adrian Carsini, in "Any Old Port in a Storm"
   c. Oscar Finch, in "Agenda for Murder"
   d. Brimmer, in "Death Lends a Hand"

4. The normally imperturbable Columbo completely loses his temper, briefly, in one emotional episode. To whom does he say, "You'd better take good care of Dr. Hidemann, because if he dies, I am going to hold you responsible."

5. At the conclusion of "Murder Under Glass," Columbo prepares a dish for Paul Gerard and himself to share with a couple of bottles of wine. Gerard tastes it, and is impressed. By this time, he realizes that the game of wits between them is over, and he will be going to prison (or worse). What back-handed compliment does he pay Columbo?

6. In "Negative Reaction," Dick Van Dyke plays a murderer who is a Pulitzer Prize-winning photographer. What ironic insult does his wife level at him when he kidnaps and ties her up, before killing her? (The irony lies in who the actor is, not in the character he plays.)

7. In "Undercover," Irving Krutch's alibi is repeatedly backed up by his girlfriend, who is a stunner. When Columbo says, skeptically, that he is always in bed with her, what does Krutch reply?
   a. "Wouldn't you be?"
   b. "Can you blame me?"
   c. "Is there a law against that?"
   d. "Can you think of something better to do?"

8. What is Columbo's second most favorite expression?
   a. "How do you like that?"
   b. "Something's been botherin' me."
   c. "You learn something new every day."
   d. "I'll keep that in mind."

9. Which irritated killer says to Columbo, "It's always one more thing. Do you have a problem with short-term memory? Perhaps you should see a physician."
   a. Col. Rumford, in "By Dawn's Early Light"
   b. Riley Greenleaf, in "Publish or Perish"
   c. Fielding Chase, in "Butterfly in Shades of Gray"
   d. Ward Fowler, in "Fade in to Murder"

10. When he arrives at the crime scene, Columbo looks and feels terrible. He had eaten some bad clams, and is carrying a bottle of Pepto Bismol in a paper bag. Taking a sip, he complains, "If the clams don't kill me, that stuff will." In what episode does this scene occur?
   a. "Strange Bedfellows"
   b. "A Trace of Murder"
   c. "Murder with Too Many Notes"
   d. "It's All in the Game"

QUIZ 10.3: RECYCLING
CAN BE FUN (!!)

"There is nothing new under the sun," according to the Bible, and certainly that is true for COLUMBO. Many clues, plot devices and motives in the NBC shows were recycled, sometimes with little change, in the ABC shows. I say, "More power to environmentally friendly television programming."

The episode list follows the questions. Except where noted, there is one NBC show and one ABC show for each question. All titles are used. Every question has only two answers (except Q. 9).

1. Which episodes feature an uncle who betrays his nephew for money? (One involves a fake kidnapping.)

2. In which episodes is the killer honored by his peers as a "Man of the Year"?

3. In which shows does the murderer finesse the police into digging up the area where he (or she) intends to hide the body, knowing that they won't dig it up again?

4. Both networks feature a character who is the owner of a professional football team. In the NBC show, he or she is the victim; in the ABC show, he or she is the killer.

5. Each network has a show in which someone is hired to investigate some sort of wrongdoing, but instead of reporting his findings to the client, he tries to blackmail the guilty party. In the NBC show, the blackmailer kills the person, who won't cooperate; in the ABC show, the blackmailer becomes a victim himself.

6. In which episodes does the victim die by suffocation in a vault while the killer is away on a trip? (Both shows were on NBC.)

7. Both networks have a character who is a magician. In the NBC episode, he is the killer; in the ABC episode, he is the victim.

8. One show on each network concerns a second victim who is killed because he or she knows about the first murder and tries to blackmail the killer (for money, not for any other advantage).

9. In three shows, someone with insight into the first murder lies to the police to cover up for the killer, and then tries to coerce him or her into a romantic relationship. (In the NBC shows, the scheme fails; in the ABC show, it succeeds.)

10. In which episodes does a victim die from hitting his or her head on a glass coffee table?

NBC EPISODES

(a) "Double Exposure"
(b) "Now You See Him..."
(c) "Murder by the Book"
(d) "Blueprint for Murder"
(e) "The Greenhouse Jungle"
(f) "Any Old Port in a Storm"
(g) "Death Lends a Hand"
(h) "The Most Crucial Game"
(i) "Try and Catch Me"

ABC EPISODES

(j) "Columbo Likes the Nightlife"
(k) "Columbo Cries Wolf"
(l) "Death Hits the Jackpot"
(m) "Ashes to Ashes"
(n) "Grand Deceptions"
(o) "A Bird in the Hand"
(p) "Columbo Goes to the Guillotine"
(q) "Columbo and the Murder of a Rock Star"

QUIZ 10.4: SUPERLATIVES, etc.

ACROSS

1. The writer of the episode that is the answer to 15 Across
7. The only episode Peter Falk directed: "_____ for Murder"
10. The writer of the most teleplays: Jackson _____
11. Jack Cassidy's character's stage name in "Now You See Him...": The Great _____
13. The last COLUMBO episode: "Columbo Likes the _____"
15. The second pilot episode: "_____ for a Dead Man"
16. The first regular season episode: "Murder by the __"
17. The last episode shown on NBC: "The _____"

19. The oldest murderer: Ruth ___
21. What the networks call a program with rotating shows
25. The only show without a murder: "No Time to __"
26. The breed of Columbo's pitiful dog: ___ hound
28. Columbo's rank on the police force
29. The only episode that Patrick McGoohan wrote, directed, and starred in: "_____ to _____" (The title has the same word twice, but the answer has it only once.)
30. "Neat and ___ " (an expression, not an episode)
31. The make of Columbo's pitiful car

DOWN

2. Columbo's favorite dish (with crackers)
3. The only episode with three murders: "A ___ in the Hand"
4. Nelson Brenner's alias in "Identity Crisis"
5. Columbo is a _____ detective
6. The actor with the most appearances as a murderer: Patrick _____
8. The initials of a webpage address
9. The city where "Dagger of the Mind" is set (and where it was partly filmed)
10. The first episode on ABC: "Columbo Goes to the _____"
11. The director of the first regular season episode: Steven _____
12. The first pilot episode: "_____: Murder"
14. The only episode Peter Falk wrote: "It's All in the ___"
18. The director of the most episodes: Vincent _____
20. The only actress to win an Emmy for COLUMBO: Faye _____
22. The setting of the show that is the answer to 23 Across
23. The youngest murderer: Fisher _____
24. The only other actress nominated for an Emmy for the show: Lee ___
27. The source of the deadly poison used in "Murder Under Glass" (a species of fish)

QUIZ 10.5: In Other Words (!)

These episode titles are fabricated, but they are roughly synonymous with the real ones. Can you identify them? [Their user ratings on the Internet Movie Database website (IMDb.com), as of Sept. 2013, are given in brackets.]

NBC EPISODES

1. "Antiquated Homicide" [6.7]

2. "Deceased Burden" [6.7]

3. "Musical Composition in Ebony" [7.3]

4. "Any Aged Haven in a Tempest" [7.8]

5. "A Question of Respect" [6.6]

6. "Unfavorable Response" [7.6]

7. "Beautiful But Deadly" [7.0]

8. "Homicide According to Bound Printed Matter" [7.4]

9. "Stiletto of the Brain" [6.8]

10. "Final Homage to the Admiral" [6.4]

11. "The Riskiest Competition" [7.2]

ABC EPISODES

12. "Peculiar Bunkmates" [6.8]

13. "The Grim Reaper Strikes It Rich" [7.2]

14. "An Avian Grasped" [6.8]

15. "Homicide, Carbon Emissions and Penumbras" [7.2]

16. "Dramatic Subterfuges" [6.6]

17. "The Lieutenant Enjoys Clubbing" [6.9]

ANSWERS
QUIZ 10.1

1. Chess Grandmaster Emmett Clayton (Laurence Harvey)
2. (c); 3. (a); 4. (d); 5. (c)
6. (b); 7. (d); 8. (a); 9. (b); 10. (a)

11. (d) The real movie, which came out in 1953 and starred Janet Leigh, was called WALKING MY BABY BACK HOME. She was also in BYE BYE BIRDIE.

12. (a)

13. (c) He makes a scratch mark on the bottle with his thumbnail at the same time.

14. (d); 15. (c); 16. (b)

17. (a) The reason, of course, is to eliminate the odor from his cigars.

18. (d); 19. (c); 20. (b)

QUIZ 10.2

1. (a); 2. (c); 3. (b)
4. Dr. Barry Mayfield, in "A Stitch in Crime"
5. He says, "I wish you had been a chef." Columbo smiles, and replies, "I understand."

6. She says that he never did have a sense of humor. For the benefit of younger readers who may not remember, he was the star of THE DICK VAN DYKE SHOW, one of the most popular situation comedies ever.

7. (a); 8. (b)
9. (c); 10. (a)

QUIZ 10.3

1. (e), (l) / 2. (f), (m)
3. (d), (k) / 4. (h), (o)
5. (g), (n) / 6. (f), (i)
7. (b), (p) / 8. (a), (j)
9. (c), (f) and (q) / 10. (g), (j)

QUIZ 10.4

1	2	3	4	5	6	7	8	9	10	11	12	13	14	15	16	17
B	O	C	H	C	O									B		S
		H		H	M	B	L	U	E	P	R	I	N	T		T
	L	I		O							R			R		E
	O	L		M		G	I	L	L	I	S			D		I
S	A	N	T	I	N	I										N
P	D			C			O		I			P				M
I	O		N	I	G	H	T	L	I	F	E	R		G		E
E	N			D	A	L						E		A		T
L				E					R	A	N	S	O	M		Z
B	O	O	K							T		C		E		
E		C	O	N	S	P	I	R	A	T	O	R	S		M	
R								N				I			C	
G	O	R	D	O	N		W	H	E	E	L	P			E	
		U			S		O		T			T			V	
G		N			T						D	I	E		E	
R	B	A	S	S	E	T		E		F		O			E	
A		W			V	L	I	E	U	T	E	N	A	N	T	
N		A			E					G					Y	
T	I	D	Y		N			P	E	U	G	E	O	T		
					S											

QUIZ 10.5

1. "Old Fashioned Murder"

2. "Dead Weight"

3. "Etude in Black"

4. "Any Old Port in a Storm"

5. "A Matter of Honor"

6. "Negative Reaction"

7. "Lovely But Lethal"

8. "Murder by the Book"

9. "Dagger of the Mind"

10. "Last Salute to the Commodore"

11. "The Most Dangerous Match"

****

12. "Strange Bedfellows"

13. "Death Hits the Jackpot"

14. "A Bird in the Hand"

15. "Murder, Smoke and Shadows"

16. "Grand Deceptions"

17. "Columbo Likes the Nightlife"

QUIZ INDEX

PART ONE: GENERAL QUESTIONS

PART TWO: BEHIND THE SCENES

PART THREE: GUEST STARS

PART FOUR: THE PLAYERS

PART FIVE: THE CHARACTERS

PART SIX: POLICE BLOTTER

PART SEVEN: THE CRIMES

PART EIGHT: THE PLOT THICKENS

PART NINE: THE INVESTIGATIONS

PART TEN: POTPOURRI

APPENDIX

REPEAT OFFENDERS

PATRICK McGOOHAN

"By Dawn's Early Light" (1974) – Col. Lyle C. Rumford
"Identity Crisis" (1975) – Nelson Brenner (or Steinmetz)
"Agenda for Murder" (1990) – Oscar Finch
"Ashes to Ashes" (1998) – Eric Prince

JACK CASSIDY

"Murder by the Book" (1971) – Ken Franklin
"Publish or Perish" (1974) – Riley Greenleaf
"Now You See Him..." (1976) – The Great Santini

ROBERT CULP

"Death Lends a Hand" (1971) – Brimmer
"The Most Crucial Game" (1972) – Paul Hanlon
"Double Exposure" (1973) – Dr. Bart Keppel

WILLIAM SHATNER

"Fade in to Murder" (1976) – Ward Fowler
"Butterfly in Shades of Grey" (1994) – Fielding Chase

GEORGE HAMILTON

"A Deadly State of Mind" (1975) – Dr. Marcus Collier
"Caution: Murder Can Be Hazardous to Your Health"
(1991) – Wade Anders

Oscar Winners on COLUMBO

(*Plays a villain on the show)

[NOTE: ONLY PERFORMERS ARE INCLUDED IN THIS LIST AND
THE EMMY WINNERS LIST.]

Edith Head – Costume Design (not a performer, but she has a
a cameo role)
Myrna Loy – Honorary Lifetime Achievement Award

Best Actor or Actress

*Jose Ferrer – CYRANO DE BERGERAC

*Ray Milland – THE LOST WEEKEND

*Faye Dunaway – NETWORK

Rod Steiger – IN THE HEAT OF THE NIGHT

Best Supporting Actor or Actress

*Martin Landau – ED WOOD

*Anne Baxter – THE RAZOR'S EDGE

*Ruth Gordon – ROSEMARY'S BABY

*Lee Grant – SHAMPOO

Kim Hunter – A STREETCAR NAMED DESIRE

Dean Jagger – TWELVE O'CLOCK HIGH

Don Ameche – COCOON

Celeste Holm – GENTLEMAN'S AGREEMENT

Emmy Winners

(*Plays a villain on the show)

Leading Roles

*Patrick McGoohan – COLUMBO ("By Dawn's Early Light" and
"Agenda for Murder")

*Faye Dunaway – COLUMBO ("It's All in the Game")

*Richard Kiley – A YEAR IN THE LIFE
THE THORN BIRDS (Supporting)

*Tyne Daly – CAGNEY AND LACEY
CHRISTY; JUDGING AMY (both Supporting)

*Rip Torn – THE LARRY SANDERS SHOW
*Dick Van Dyke – THE DICK VAN DYKE SHOW
*Ruth Gordon - TAXI
*Lee Grant – THE NEON CEILING; PEYTON PLACE (Supporting)

Mariette Hartley – THE INCREDIBLE HULK
William Windom – MY WORLD AND WELCOME TO IT
Rue McClanahan – THE GOLDEN GIRLS
Julie Harris – VICTORIA REGINA; LITTLE MOON OF ALBAN
Gena Rowlands – THE BETTY FORD STORY; FACE OF A
STRANGER / HYSTERICAL BLINDNESS
(Supporting)

Supporting Roles

*Ian Buchanan – THE BOLD AND THE BEAUTIFUL
*William Shatner – BOSTON LEGAL
*Dabney Coleman – SWORN TO SILENCE
*Robert Vaughn – WASHINGTON BEHIND CLOSED DOORS
Blythe Danner – HUFF
Pat Harrington, Jr. – ONE DAY AT A TIME
Richard Dysart – L. A. LAW

NOTES

Printed in Poland
by Amazon Fulfillment
Poland Sp. z o.o., Wrocław

51653370R00105